BASIC ILLUSTRATED
MEDICINAL PLANTS

BASIC ILLUSTRATED
MEDICINAL PLANTS

Jim Meuninck

FALCONGUIDES

GUILFORD, CONNECTICUT
HELENA, MONTANA

AN IMPRINT OF ROWMAN & LITTLEFIELD

FALCONGUIDES®

An imprint of Rowman & Littlefield
Falcon, FalconGuides, and Outfit Your Mind are registered trademarks of Rowman & Littlefield.

Distributed by NATIONAL BOOK NETWORK

British Library Cataloguing-in-Publication Information available

Library of Congress Cataloging-in-Publication Data

Meuninck, Jim, 1942- author.
 Basic illustrated medicinal plants / Jim Meuninck.
   pages cm — (Basic illustrated series)
  ISBN 978-0-7627-9191-0 (paperback)
 1. Medicinal plants—United States—Identification. 2. Medicinal plants—United States—Pictorial works.
I. Title.
 QK98.5.U6M484 2014
 581.6'34—dc23
                                                                           2014027446

∞™ The paper used in this publication meets the minimum requirements of American National Standard for Information Sciences—Permanence of Paper for Printed Library Materials, ANSI/NISO Z39.48-1992.

CONTENTS

Introduction ix

How to Use This Guide x

    Kitchen Science: General Principles of Preparing Medicinal Plants x

    Safety and Efficacy Documents xii

    Medicinal and Edible Plants xii

Chapter One: Medicinal Plants of the West 1

Chapter Two: Medicinal Plants of Forests East and West 15

Chapter Three: Medicinal Plants of Wetlands 29

Chapter Four: Medicinal Plants of Yards, Prairies, Roadsides, and

Meadows 47

Appendix A: My Top Eleven Edible Garden Herbs 73

Appendix B: Helpful Websites 74

Appendix C: References and Resources 75

Index 81

About the Author 84

ACKNOWLEDGMENTS

I want to thank Dr. James Duke for his ground breaking references found online, in field guides and medicinal plants handbooks presenting user friendly and innovative advice. Thanks also go to Jill, my steadfast companion, best friend, and spouse. A special nod to daughter Rebecca, who has accomplished so much for all of us through her hard work at the Ann Arbor Ecology Center, and once again, I thank my ancestors and yours for their contributions to the vast amount of botanical knowledge that improves our diet and engenders good health.

This book would not be possible without all the efforts and insights of the FalconGuides team to include my gracious, creative, intelligent, and hard-working editor, David LeGere. Accolades galore for Staci Zacharski, editor-extraordinaire who hammered home this book's form and guided it to completion. And thanks to both copyeditor, Kathy Brook and proofreader, Paulette Baker, and to layout artist, Melissa Evarts for her wonderful creativity.

INTRODUCTION

Robust health and longevity require a judicious and objective approach to medicinal herbs and plant nutrition. Our ancestors found a medicinal use for every plant, and those foraging skills link our history on the planet. Borrowing from their evolutionary wisdom, a successful forager can select what is needed and what to eliminate. The purpose of this book is to provide you with the knowledge to make informed choices about what works and what does not. But here's the problem: Many herbalists and herb purveyors use a reductionist approach to disease treatment. Like modern allopathic medicine, they target illness with a single plant chemical or an arsenal of potent chemicals in combination. There is a place for this; that place too often is in the late stages of disease. What I advocate is prevention: Eat good-quality whole foods, drink pure water, exercise daily—and add selected medicinal plants to your diet. This healthy regimen prevents disease by nipping it in the bud. Bear in mind, however, when using the term *medicinal herb* I am most likely talking about an edible wild plant, too—they are often the same thing. This fact lends credence to the old saw: You are what you eat. You are a plant with wheels because, either directly or indirectly, all of your chemistry comes from plant chemistry—therefore plants are your food and medicine.

Understand, also, a healthy person eats the foods that are in season—the plants of spring, summer, autumn, and winter. These seasonal plants provide what is right for that time of year. Spring provides the immune-enhancing tonic greens: nettles, alliums, watercress, and dock. Summer provides the antioxidant-rich cancer-fighting fruits and berries, and autumn, the fiber-rich pomes, seeds, and polysaccharides that give us energy and strength to thrive through the cold months of winter. Formed in the breast of nature, these natural foods and plant medicines are free and available to those who know. With this book you will become one of those who know.

My nutritional beliefs are the accumulation of knowledge from numerous sources: from experience, science, undergraduate and graduate school, hundreds of books, other experts, gardening, foraging, and personal use. A broad base of whole plant foods and herbs make the foundation of healthy diet and pave the road to longevity.

With all that said, I am delighted to share these pages, my humble contribution to the human experience. Let's go walk the planet, pull some weeds, and have fun!

HOW TO USE THIS GUIDE

First thumb through the book, look at the pictures, and let your curiosity explore. After this initial voyage, check out the section called My Top Eleven Edible Garden Herbs (p. 73). These are easy to identify, universally distributed, potent herbs that you can introduce to your garden and diet.

Next, because you bought this field guide for a reason, seek the plants that resolve your questions. Use the index to find the common name, then page to the plant and continue your odyssey.

This field guide's unique identification system moves the forager from environment to environment. It reveals the benefits of familiar plants as well as the rare and complex. It builds from a solid foundation of basic information and then provides resources for the forager to go as far as he or she wants to go. The goal is to identify for the reader medicinal plants that have documented benefits and a long history of traditional use. It helps you find the herb in its habitat and harvest it in an environmentally safe and sustainable way.

Entries begin with **Identification**—a summary of the plant's physical characteristics to aid in plant discovery, followed by an explanation of the typical **Habitat** and section of the country where the plant is found.

Next the plant's modern **Food** and **Traditional uses** are discussed, including American Indian and pioneer uses.

Throughout the book, you will discover which herbs are beneficial and which are potentially dangerous.

The **Medicinal uses** section uncovers safe and proven herbs that nudge the body in the right direction and initiate subtle changes—many are medicinal food—whereas other herbs described are powerful and reserved for the skilled practitioner. This field guide helps you discover the difference.

In the **Notes** I share experiences, skills, gardening tips, and some recipes gleaned from my forty-plus years exploring the plant world.

Read each **CAUTION** carefully to discover the plant's dangerous characteristics.

The plant research citations provide a wealth of supplemental websites, books, and research references. You'll find this useful information in the appendixes.

Kitchen Science: General Principles of Preparing Medicinal Plants

Many of the wild plants described in this book are edible and medicinal. To capture their health-protecting chemistry, eat them as food. However, when the desired result is a concentration of chemistry from one or a combination of plants, specific techniques render optimum results. The following describes various ways to release plant chemistry. It is simple. Let's call it kitchen science.

Infusions or teas are prepared by pouring hot water (just off the boil) over fresh or dried herbs. This process pulls the water-soluble fraction from the plants. Typically, the soft parts (leaves and flowering parts) of the plant are infused. *Examples:* dandelion leaf tea, nettle leaf tea, mint leaf tea, bee balm flower tea. *Amount:* 1 teaspoon dried herb to 1 cup of water; 4 teaspoons of fresh herb to 1 cup of water. Cover the steeping pot until infusion reaches a drinkable temperature.

Decoction is an extraction made by simmering or boiling herbs in water. Decoctions pull water-soluble chemistry from the hard parts of the plant: the stems, seeds, bark, and roots. *Example:* wild leek soup or a dandelion root decoction. *Amount:* 1 teaspoon dried herb to 1 cup of water; 4 teaspoons fresh herb to 1 cup of water. Simmer until you achieve the desired concentration—typically, the longer you simmer, the stronger the extraction.

Percolation is the dripping of water or alcohol through a damp mass of powdered herb. Chop or grind the herb, gather it in a coffee filter, and then drip water, alcohol, or a combination of both through the herb to release the chemistry. Water releases the hydrophilic or water-soluble fraction, whereas alcohol releases the lipophilic or fat-soluble chemistry. *Example:* dripping hot water and alcohol through fresh-ground golden seal root, or dripping hot water through ground cayenne to release capsaicin. *Amount:* 100 ml of liquid through 10 g dried herb, or a multiple of those proportions. Repeat the process over and over to increase concentration.

Tinctures require chopping and blending an herb in alcohol; other chemicals, such as apple cider vinegar or glycerin, are suitable alternatives. Facilitate maceration (blending) with a food processor or blender. *Example:* Blend 100 proof alcohol with fresh echinacea flowers. Cut the whole flowers in small pieces, add leaves, place all in a blender, cover with 100 proof alcohol (ethanol) and macerate. Let the maceration rest in the refrigerator for 4 hours, then strain (I squeeze the drug from the mass through clean panty hose or cheesecloth), and bottle. *Amount:* When making a tincture with a dry herb, typically a 1:5 ratio is used—that is, 1 ounce of the dried herb is macerated and blended with 5 ounces of 50% (100 proof) alcohol. With fresh herbs a 1:2 ratio is often used—1 g to every ml of 50% (100 prooof) alcohol.

Fomentation is the application of a warm or cool herb decoction or infusion with a clean cotton cloth to an injury on the body. Dip the cloth into the decoction then wrap it wet around the target area. *Example:* Dip a cloth in a cold infusion of crushed jewelweed and apply it to the poison ivy–inflamed skin. *Amount:* enough to saturate cloth and cover the area to be treated.

Poultice is made by pounding and macerating fresh herbs and applying the moist herb mass directly over a body part. *Example:* Put a warm, wet, and pounded mass of plantain over a wound. *Amount:* large enough amount to cover area to be treated.

Capsule powders are dried and finely ground herb loaded into a 00 size capsule. *Example:* Many phyto-pharmaceutical companies prepare over-the-counter dried herbs in 00 capsules. .

Oils and salves are dried or fresh herbs cooked in oil to extract the active principle. Strain the oil through a filter (cheesecloth, new sock, or the like) and then thicken the warm oil with melted beeswax. *Example:* Cook the aerial parts (leaves, flowers) of yarrow, strain, then apply to wounds and abrasions. The cooled blend is a practical first-aid wound treatment. *Amount:* With yarrow I lightly pack a pan with fresh leaves and flowers and cover with olive oil or lard (German studies suggest lard is better absorbed through human skin than plant oils).

Safety and Efficacy Documents

Throughout this field guide I document proven efficacy and safety with numerous science-based references including this shorthand: (CM), (GR), (WHO), and (NIH).

(CM) is documentation and research gleaned from Canada Natural Health Product Monographs—250 PDF files on medicinal herbs and other natural health products available free of charge online at http://webprod.hc-sc.gc.ca/nhpid-bdipsn/monosReq.do?lang=eng.

(GR) refers to the United States Agriculture Research Service and Dr. Jim Duke's database, where plants are catalogued for chemical constituents and ethnobotanical uses (www.ars-grin.gov/duke/).

(WHO) refers to the World Health Organization collection of scientific and documented medicinal herbs online at http://whqlibdoc.who.int/publications/1999/9241545178.pdf.

(NIH) refers to the list of medicinal herbs at the National Institutes of Health's Office of Dietary Supplements l, k (http://ods.od.nih.gov/factsheets/list-all/).

This wealth of information helps support the traditional and modern uses of the medicinal plants covered in this field guide.

Medicinal and Edible Plants

Here is a short guide to medicinal and edible plants that broaden your diet and increase the amount of available nutrients and phytochemistry for optimum health.

Bee balm blossoms (summer, blossoms), p. 49

Black walnuts (fall, nuts), p. 16

Blueberry (summer, fruit and leaves [as tea]), p. 30

Burdock (peel and slice summer or fall root and sauté), p. 50

Cranberry (fall, fresh-cooked leaves and dried fruit), p. 33

Dandelions (spring, leaves in salad, root in decoction), p. 54

Duckweed (summer, cleaned and sautéed or put in soups), p. 34

Elderberry (fritter the flowers and make jelly from summer bounty), p. 36

Evening primrose (fall flowers in salad and winter seeds in bread, pancakes, etc.), p. 56

Jewelweed (fall flowers in salads), p. 37

Lemon balm (leaf tea in every season: cold or hot infusion), p. 48

Mint (spring, summer, and fall leaves and flowers as flavoring or tea), p. 39

Plantain (spring and summer leaves in salad or wrapped around grains and other fillings), p. 66

Stinging nettle (leaves in any season as tea, sautéed, or added to soups and stews) p. 69

Watercress (in every season add leaves and stems in soup, egg dishes, or grill), p. 43

Yellow dock (spring leaves and new summer growth torn from midrib and added to salads and sautéed), p. 53

Chapter One:
Medicinal Plants of the West

Here are a number of medicinal plants found in states west of the Mississippi and primarily in the Mountain West.

Arnica (Arnica), 2

Arrowleaf Balsamroot (Balsamorhiza), 3

Bistort (Persicaria), 4

Cascara Sagrada (Cascara), 5

Devil's Club (Oplopanax), 5

Douglas Fir (Pseudotsuga), 6

Ephedra (Ephedra), 7

Juniper (Juniperus), 8

Oregon Grape (Mahonia), 9

Red Alder (Alnus), 10

Red Cedar (Thuja), 11

Sage (Artemesia), 12

Sitka Valerian (Valeriana), 13

Yew (Taxus), 14

ARNICA, MOUNTAIN TOBACCO, LEOPARD'S BANE, WOLF'S BANE

Asteraceae *(Arnica montana* L.; *A. acaulis* Walt; *A. cordifolia* Hook; *A. latifolia* Bong.)*

Heartleaf arnica

Identification: Perennial that grows to 18". Rhizome is brownish. Leaves form a basal rosette. Hairy stem rises from the rosette and has 2–6 smaller leaves, ovate to lance shaped and somewhat dentate (toothed). Terminal yellow flowers emerge from the axil of the top pair of leaves. Flowers are 2"–3" in diameter and have a hairy receptacle and hairy calyx. Tiny disk flowers reside inside the corolla and are tubular; there are as many as 100 of these disk flowers per flower head. Some variation between species.

Habitat: Typically in the shady mountainous areas, along seeps and stream banks to 10,000', and in wet alpine meadows.

Food: Not edible; toxic—internal consumption causes stomach pain, vomiting, and diarrhea. High doses may induce cardiac arrest.

Traditional uses: Flowers and roots have been used to treat bruises; to relieve sprains, arthritic pain, muscle ache; to heal chapped lips; and to treat acne. Volatile oils in the flowers used in making perfume. Native Americans used an infusion of the roots externally for back pain. A poultice was used on edemas to reduce swelling. The plant was considered anthelmintic, antiseptic, astringent, choleretic, emmenagogue, expectorant, febrifuge, stimulant, and tonic, and was used as a topical agent for wound healing. The whole plant, used after extraction in ointment or as a compress, has antimicrobial and fungicidal action. In folk medicine, the plant was used to induce abortions.

Modern uses: Arnica preparations include tinctures, salves, lotions, and crushed or bruised plant placed externally on arthritis, bruises, muscle sprains, and strains. Theoretically, healing or comfort is induced by improving circulation to injured area. Commission E, the German compendium of therapeutic herbs for human use, approves arnica preparations for treating fevers, colds, skin inflammations, coughs, bronchitis, mouth and pharynx inflammations, rheumatism, injuries, and tendencies toward infection (weakened immunity). Medicinal parts include the roots and rhizome, dried flowers, and leaves collected before flowering. Because of the toxic nature of the plant, homeopathic doses are used to manage pain, to treat diabetic retinopathy, and to treat muscle soreness. The plant extract is used in antidandruff preparations and hair tonics. In a few clinical trials, arnica presents mixed results as an anti-inflammatory. Other studies show it may be an effective anti-inflammatory and may reduce pain after exercise (see Memorial Sloan Kettering 2014).

Notes: Arnica species are abundant in the Mountain West from the Little Bighorns through the Rockies and on into the Pacific Northwest. They are numerous in and around the slopes of Mount Rainier, Mount Adams, and Mount Baker in the Cascades of Washington State.

CAUTION: Flowers may be a skin irritant, causing skin reddening or eczema. Do not use during pregnancy. Do not use if sensitive (allergic) to members of the daisy family. Health-care practitioners warn not to use arnica on mucous membranes, open skin wounds, or the eyes. Do not use orally except in homeopathic concentrations. Arnica may interact with anticoagulants and induce bleeding.

ARROWLEAF BALSAMROOT

Asteraceae *(Balsamorhiza sagittata* Pursh Nutt.*)*

Identification: Leaves are basal with a thick, tough petiole, arrow-point shaped, hairy, and rough to the touch, 8"–20" in length. Flowers are yellow, long stalked. Up to 22 yellow rays encircle the yellow disk of florets. Whole plant is 1'–2' in height.

Habitat: Along banks and dry washes of foothills and higher elevation of the Rockies from Colorado to British Columbia on dry, sunny slopes.

Food: Young leaves and shoots are edible, as well as young flower stalks and young stems. They may be steamed or eaten raw. Peeled roots are edible but are bitter

Arrowleaf balsamroot

unless slow-cooked to break down the indigestible polysaccharide (inulin). The roots may be cooked and dried, then reconstituted in simmering water before eating. Pound seeds into a meal to use as flour or eat out of hand. The roasted seeds can be ground into pinole. The Nez Perce Indians roasted and ground the seeds, which they then formed into little balls by adding grease.

Traditional uses: Native Americans used the wet leaves as a wound dressing and a poultice over burns. The sticky sap sealed wounds and was considered antiseptic. Although balsam root is bitter when peeled and eaten, it contains inulin that may stimulate the immune system, providing protection from acute sickness such as colds and flu. The sap was considered antibacterial and antifungal. A decoction of the leaves, stems, and roots was sipped as therapy for stomachaches and colds. The root also used for treating gonorrhea and syphilis. In the sweat lodge, balsam root smoke and steam were reported to relieve headaches. The smoke from this powerful male warrior plant used in smudging ceremonies to cleanse a person or thing of the evil that makes them sick. It is also a disinfectant and inhaled for body aches. The chewed root applied as a poultice over sores, wounds, and burns.

Modern uses: Powdered root may be antifungal and can be applied as a poultice or salve to treat tinea cruris irritations (jock itch) and athlete's foot. Dry root tincture in warm water or juice appears to soothe sore throats (anecdotal evidence). Plant is little studied or used in any modern scientifically proven context. Traditional uses still practiced.

Notes: Balsam root is widespread in the Bitterroots and other Idaho wilderness areas. In a pinch—should you get lost in these vast mountainous expanses—here is a food that helps you survive. But freeing the root, often deeply and intricately woven into the rock, is an exhausting task.

Bistort

BISTORT, MEADOW BISTORT, ALPINE BISTORT
Polygonaceae *(Persicaria bistortoides* **Pursh.;** *P. vivaparum* **L.***)*
Status of genus is in flux; the plants may also be cited as Polygonum.

Identification: Perennial to 30" with basal leaves and a few smaller leaves produced near lower end of flowering stem. The leaves are oblong-ovate or triangular-ovate in shape and narrow at the base. Petioles are broadly winged. White flowers form from a single dense cluster atop erect stalk, later forming a seed head with brownish achenes (seeds). Blooms from late spring into autumn, producing tall stems ending in single terminal racemes that are club-like spikes.

Habitat: Both species grow from New Mexico to Alaska on wet, open slopes and are abundant in the alpine meadows of Mount Rainier and the Cascades. Visit the nature center garden at Sunrise (the northeast entrance at Mount Raineer) to see this plant and other Northwest medicinals.

Food: Young leaves and shoots are edible raw or cooked. They have a slightly sour taste. Older leaves are tough and stringy. Use leaves in salads and cooked with meat. The starchy root is edible; boil in soups and stews, or soak in water, dry, and grind into flour for biscuits, rolls, and bread. The cooked roots taste like almonds or chestnuts. The seeds are edible and pleasant tasting.

Traditional uses: This vitamin C–rich plant was used to treat or prevent scurvy. The tincture is astringent and used externally on cuts, abrasions, acne, insect stings and bites, inflammations, and infections.

Modern uses: Bistort contains tannins that can help improve diarrhea and mouth and throat irritation by reducing swelling (inflammation) (see McGuffin et al.1997). Little used today as a medicinal. Traditional uses still employed by montane-dwelling Native Americans and Europeans.

Note: Easily identified and gathered in areas where harvesting is allowed.

CASCARA SAGRADA, BUCKTHORN

Rhamnaceae *(Rhamnus alnifolia* (L.) Her.; *R. purshiana* (DC.) Cooper)

Cascara sagrada

Identification: Bush or small tree grows 4′–20′ tall. Has many branches, thornless, densely foliated; when mature the bark is grayish brown with gray-white lenticels. Leaves are thin, hairy on the ribs, fully margined, elliptical to ovate, 2″ in length. Greenish-white flowers are numerous and grow on axillary cymes. Flowers are very small with 5 petals. The ripe fruit is red to black purple with 2 or 3 seeds. *R. purshiana* is taller, to 30′, a Western species, with leaves that have 20–24 veins. White flowers are in clusters.

Habitat: *R. purshiana:* Foothills of British Columbia, Idaho, Washington, Montana, and Oregon. A lesser known and little used species, *R. alnifolia*, grows throughout the dunes of Lake Michigan and other Great Lake dune areas.

Food: Not edible.

Traditional uses: Prior to World War II, cascara tablets were available over the counter as a laxative. Native Americans used the bark infusion as a purgative, laxative, and worm-killing tea. An infusion of the twigs and fruit was used as an emetic.

Modern uses: The bark extract is a powerful laxative and Commission E–approved for treating constipation. Bark infusion is a cleansing tonic, but chronic, continuous use may be carcinogenic. Use only under the care of a physician, holistic or otherwise. The laxative response may last 8 hours.

Notes: A naturopathic physician once laced my salmon with cascara extract, a practical joke. Berries from a *Rhamnus* species in the Midwest once ruined an anniversary dinner. These berries can be mistaken for edible fruit with rueful consequences.

DEVIL'S CLUB

Aralioideae *(Oplopanax horridus* Sm. Torr.; Gray es. Miq*)*

Identification: Shrubby, spiny, big-leafed perennial to 10′. Spreading, crooked, and tangled growth covered with thorns. Wood has sweet odor. Dinner plate–size maple-like leaves armed underneath with thorns. Club-like flower head has white flowers grouped in a compact terminal head. Berries shiny, bright red, flattened.

Devil's club

Habitat: Found in coastal mountains and coastline of the northwestern United States and Canada. Seepage sites, stream banks, moist low-lying forested areas, old avalanche tracks. Typically grows at low altitude, but in Canada it may grow to the tree line.

Food: Not often eaten as food, its berries are inedible. According to Moerman (1998), spring buds boiled and eaten by the Oweekeno tribe.

Traditional uses: Related to ginseng, devil's club's roots, berries, and especially the greenish inner bark are some of the most important medicinal plants of West Coast Native Americans used in rituals and medicine. Berries rubbed into hair to kill lice or add shine. The inner bark chewed raw as purgative and emetic or taken with hot water for the same purpose. Inner bark infused or decocted to treat stomach and bowel cramps, arthritis, stomach ulcers, and other unspecified illnesses of the digestive system. Root, leaves, and stems added to hot baths and sweat lodges to treat arthritis. The cooked and shredded root bark used as a poultice for many skin conditions. The stem decoction used for reducing fever. Tea from inner bark used for treating diabetes, a common ailment in aboriginal people who now eat a fatty and carbohydrate-rich Western diet. The dried root mixed with tobacco and smoked to treat headache. An infusion of crushed stems used as a blood purifier. Stem ashes and oil used on skin ailments. Traditional use as an abortifacient is disproven.

Modern uses: Scientific consensus reports devil's club as hypoglycemic. There is a long history of use by Native Americans to treat adult-onset diabetes. Extracts from the inner bark are antibiotic, specifically against the bacterium genus *Mycobacterium* that causes tuberculosis (see: http://cms.herbalgram.org/herbalgram/issue62/article2697.html). German clinical trials show the plant has anti-inflammatory and analgesic activity. Animal studies show that a methanolic extract of the roots reduces blood pressure and heart rate (Circosta et al. 1994).

Notes: Native Americans burned devil's club, then mixed the ashes with grease to make a black face paint that was said to give a warrior supernatural power. Bella Coola used the spiny sticks as protective charms. And they scraped bark boiled with grease to make dye. Other Native American hunters sponged a decoction of the plant's bark over their body to remove human odor—a strategy still in use today.

DOUGLAS FIR

Pinaceae (*Pseudotsuga menziesii* Mirbel Franco)

Identification: Medium to large conifer with narrow, pointed crown, slightly drooping branches (deeply furrowed bark on mature trees), and straight trunk. Coastal variety grows to 240'. Single flat needle, pointed but soft ended, about 1" long, are evenly spaced along the twigs. Cones to 4" have winged seeds, 3 pointed bracts extending beyond cone scales look like the legs and rear end of a mouse hiding in the cone; distinctive (see photo).

Habitat: Mountain West and West Coast, from Mexico north to British Columbia; grows best on wet, well-drained slopes.

Food: Shoot tips are used to flavor foods and made into a tea. Pitch chewed as a breath cleanser. Rare Douglas fir sugar accumulates on the ends of branch tips of trees found in sunny exposures on mid-summer days—sugar candy looks like whitish frostlike globules.

Pseudotsuga menziesii

Traditional uses: This was and is a popular and important sweat lodge plant. Its aromatic needled branches are steamed to treat rheumatism and in cleansing purification rituals. Buds, bark, leaves, new-growth end sprouts, and pitch all used as medicine by Native Americans. A decoction of buds is unproven treatment for venereal diseases. Bark infusion taken to treat bowel and stomach

"Mice" hiding in a Douglas fir cone

problems. The ashes of burned bark was mixed with water to treat diarrhea. Needle infusion said to relieve paralysis. Leaves made into tea to treat arthritic complaints. Pitch used to seal wounds and chewed like gum to treat sore throat; considered an effective first aid for cuts and abrasions, bites, and stings. Decoction of new-growth twigs, shoots, needles used to treat colds. Ashes of twigs and bark mixed with fat to treat rheumatic arthritis.

Modern uses: Important ritual plant in Native American spiritual rites; many traditional uses still employed.

Notes: Excellent firewood for cooking fish and meat. Also a top-ranked lumber tree used to make clear veneer plywood.

EPHEDRA, MORMAN TEA, JOINT FIR, MA HUANG
Ephedraceae *(Ephedra viridis* Coville*; E. sinica* Stapf)*

Identification: There are several Joint-fir species. *E. viridis* looks like it has lost all its leaves. It is a yellow-green plant, many jointed and twiggy, 1'–4' tall, with small leaf scales and double-seeded cones in the fall.

Habitat: Various species are found on dry rocky soil, sand, or desertlike areas of the United States: Utah, Arizona, western New Mexico, Colorado, Nevada, California, and Oregon. Numerous plants discovered on route to the top of Fifty Mile Plateau in Utah.

Mormon tea

Ephedra sinica *(Photo by author taken at Beall Garden, Michigan State University)*

Food: Native Americans infused the roasted seeds. Roasted and ground seeds were also mixed with corn or wheat flour to make fried mush.

Traditional uses: *E. viridis* (Mormon tea) used in infusion as a tonic and laxative; to treat anemia, colds, ulcers, and backache; to stem diarrhea; and as therapy for the kidneys and bladder. The decoction or infusion considered a cleansing tonic (blood purifier). Dried and powdered stems used externally to treat wounds and sores. The moistened powder applied to burns. Native American women used the plant to stimulate delayed menstrual flow (dysmenorrhea). Seeds roasted before being brewing into tea.

Modern uses: The Chinese powder *E. sinica* and use it to treat coughs and bronchitis, bronchial asthma, congestion, hay fever, and obesity. It is an appetite suppressant and basal metabolism stimulant. Active alkaloids are ephedrine and pseudoephedrine, which increase body heat, stimulate heart rate, restrict blood vessels, and make breathing easier by expanding bronchial tubes (NIH). American ephedra is available as a tea or in capsules over the counter and but has little or no vasoactive effects.

CAUTION: Ephedra is a precursor in the illicit manufacture of methamphetamine. *E. sinica*, as a cardiovascular stimulant and central nervous system stimulant, may be dangerous to people with elevated blood pressure, heart disease, and/or tachycardia. The drug is federally regulated and not to be used during pregnancy or by nursing mothers. Numerous drug interactions documented, including death. The import and use of this drug is restricted in several countries. Deaths have been associated with its abuse.

JUNIPER

Cupressaceae *(Juniperus communis* L.*)*

Identification: Evergreen tree to 50′ or low-lying spreading shrub; often grows in colonies. It has flat needles in whorls of 3, spreading from the branches. Leaves are evergreen, pointy, stiff, somewhat flattened, and light green. Buds covered with scalelike needles. Berries are blue, hard, and when scraped with a fingernail emit a tangy smell and impart a tangy flavor—a somewhat creosote-like taste. Male flowers are catkin-like with numerous stamens in 3 segmented whorls; female flowers are green and oval.

Habitat: Nationwide on mountain slopes, forests, dune lands.

Food: Dried berries cooked with game and fowl. Place berry in a pepper mill or grate into bean soup, lamb stew, wild game, and domestic fowl. For tea, crush 2 berries and add them to water just off the boil. Gin, vodka, schnapps, and aquavit are flavored with juniper berries. Use berries in grilling marinades. Be judicious: Large amounts of the berry may be toxic; use in small amounts like a spice.

Juniper berries

Traditional uses: The diluted essential oil applied to the skin to draw out impurities and cleanse deeper skin tissue. It has been used to promote menstruation and to relieve PMS and dysmenorrhea. Traditional practitioners use 1 teaspoon of berries to 1 cup of water, boil for 3 minutes, let steep until cool. A few practitioners add bark and needles to berry tea. The berry considered an antiseptic, a diuretic, a tonic, and a digestive aid.

Modern uses: Mice trials suggest the berry extract in pharmaceutical doses to be anti-inflammatory, at least in the rodents. Juniper oil used successfully as a diuretic and may be useful as adjunct therapy for diabetes (GR). Commission E–approved for treating dyspepsia. The berry is diuretic, and so the extract is diuretic (Odrinil Water Pill) and therefore indicated for treating heart disease, high blood pressure, and dropsy. The berry extract is used in Europe to treat arthritis and gout. Animal studies of the extract in various combinations showed anti-inflammatory and anti-cancer activity, but this is unproven in human trials. It decreased glycemic levels in diabetic rats. In human trials, the berry extract combined with nettle and yarrow extracts failed to prevent gingivitis. Juniper oil and wintergreen oil (30 ml of Kneipp-Rheumabad) may be added to bath water to reduce pain.

Notes: Chew on a berry; ripe, soft ones are tastiest. Add 5 berries to duck, goose, lamb, venison, or goat stew and heighten the flavor adventure.

CAUTION: It's used as an antiseptic for urinary tract problems and gallbladder complaints but contraindicated in the presence of kidney disease; do not use if kidney infection or kidney disease is suspected. Pregnant women should avoid this herb because it may induce uterine contractions. It may increase menstrual bleeding. Do not use the concentrated and caustic essential oil internally without guidance from a licensed holistic health-care practitioner.

OREGON GRAPE

Berberidaceae *(Mahonia aquifolium* (Pursh) Nutt.; *M. nervosa* Pursh Nutt. var. *nervosa)*

Identification: *Mahonia aquifolium* is an evergreen shrub growing to 6′ tall with a gray stem and holly-like, shiny leaves that are pinnate, compound with pointed edges. Small, bright yellow flower; waxy, deep blue berries. Roots and root hairs, when peeled, are bright yellow inside due to the alkaloid berberine. *M. nervosa* is a

Mahonia nervosa

smaller forest dweller with rosette of compound leaves in a whorl up to 3' tall, berries on central spikes. **Habitat:** Find *M. nervosa* along Mount Baker Highway in Washington State. Also in open forests and graveyards. *M. aquifolium* is found in Washington State and east into Idaho and Montana along roadsides and forest edges.

Food: Natives of the Northwest eat the tart berries of *M. aquifolium* in late summer. Native Americans smashed the berries and dried them for later use. They may be boiled into jam, but be certain to add honey or sugar because the juice is tart. Carrier Indians of the Northwest simmered the young leaves and ate them. The smaller, creeping *M. nervosa* is prepared and eaten in the same way, and is preferred, but it is not as abundant. Try berries mixed with other fruit to improve the taste. Berries also are pounded into paste, formed into cakes, and dried for winter food.

Traditional uses: When eaten raw in small amounts, the fruit is slightly emetic. Tart berries of both species are considered a morning-after pick-me-up. These two species of bitter and astringent herbs used to treat liver and gallbladder complaints. The bark infusion used by Native Americans as an eyewash. According to traditional use, the decocted drug from the inner bark (berberine) stimulates the liver and gallbladder, cleansing them, releasing toxins, and increasing the flow of bile. The bark and root decoction reportedly was used externally for treating staphylococcus infections. According to Michael Moore (2003), the drug stimulates thyroid function and is used to treat diarrhea and gastritis. According to Deni Brown (1995), *M. aquifolium* has been used to treat chronic hepatitis and dry type eczema. Blackfoot used root decoction of *M. aquifolium* to stem hemorrhaging. Root also used in decoction to treat upset stomach and other stomach problems.

Modern uses: *M. aquifolium* extractions are available in commercial ointments to treat dry skin, unspecified rashes, and psoriasis. The bitter drug may prove an appetite stimulant, but little research supports this hypothesis. Other unproven uses in homeopathic doses include the treatment of liver and gallbladder problems.

Notes: Simmer the shredded bark and roots of both species in water to make a bright yellow dye.

CAUTION: Do not use during pregnancy.

RED ALDER
Betulaceae *(Alnus rubra Bong.)*
Identification: Member of the birch family that grows to 80' in height, often much smaller. Bark smooth and gray when young, coarse and whitish gray when mature. *A. rubra* bark turns red to orange when exposed to moisture. Leaves are bright green, oval, coarsely toothed, and pointed. Male flowers clustered in long hanging catkins; female seed capsule is ovoid cone. Small, slightly winged, flat seed nuts.
Habitat: Species ranges from California to Alaska, and east to Idaho in moist areas.

Food: Members of this genus provide a generous resource of firewood in the Northwest for savory barbecue cooking. The bark and wood chips are preferred over mesquite for smoking fish, especially salmon. Scrape the sweet inner bark in the early spring and eat fresh, or combine with flour to make cakes.

Traditional uses: Sweat lodge floors often covered in alder leaf, and switches of alder used for applying water to the body and the hot rocks; alder ashes used as

Alder

a paste for brushing teeth with a chewing stick. Cones of subspecies *A. sinuata* also used for medicine, as are other alder species. The smashed pulp of catkins is an oral cathartic (to help move the bowels). Bark mixed with other plants in decoction used as a tonic. Female catkins used in decoction to treat gonorrhea. A poultice of leaves applied to skin wounds and skin infections. In the Okanagan area of central Washington and British Columbia, Native Americans used an infusion of new-end shoots as an appetite stimulant for children. The leaf tea infusion is said to be an itch- and inflammation-relieving wash for insect bites and stings, poison ivy, and poison oak. Upper Tanana informants reported that a decoction of the inner bark reduces fever. An infusion of bark used to wash sores, cuts, and wounds.

Modern uses: This is still an important warrior plant in sweat lodge ceremonies. For more on sweat lodges, see the DVD *Native American Medicine and Little Medicine* (Meuninick, Clark, and Roman 2007). Black alder, *A. glutinosa*, is endemic to the Northern Hemisphere and used in Russia as a gargle to relieve sore throat and reduce fever. Research on betulin and lupeol in alder shows it may inhibit tumor growth (www.ncbi.nlm.nih.gov/pmc/articles/PMC2764818/).

Notes: To smoke meat with alder, soak the wood chips overnight in water, then place the moist chips on coals or charcoal to smoke meat. In 1961 I saw more than one hundred Native Americans smoking fish, moose, and caribou for winter storage along a 10-mile stretch of the Denali Highway in Alaska. Hunting rules at that time required any person shooting a caribou to give some of the meat to the First Peoples, who preserved it for winter food. They filleted fish, stabbed them on a stick, and smoked them over a smoldering alder fire. Ashes of alder mixed with tobacco and smoked. In hardwood-poor areas of western North America, alder burns slower than pine and is a suitable home-heating fuel. Bark is stripped and soaked in water to make an orange to rust-colored dye. Find numerous alder species across North America, often in impenetrable mazes surrounding streambeds—great bear habitat, so be careful.

RED CEDAR

Cupressaceae *(Thuja plicata D. Don.)*

Identification: Tall, aromatic evergreen tree. Many branched from the trunk skyward. Needles flattened; dark green above, lighter green below. Heavy seed crops produced every 3 years. Fertility reached at about 20 years of age.

Habitat: Windward side of the Cascades, including Vancouver Island and the Olympic Peninsula, and in northern Idaho—moist bottomland with deep rich soils.

Food: *T. plicata*'s primary use is and was for making cooking boxes and planks for flavoring and cooking salmon. The cambium (inner bark) could be eaten as a survival food, but there are numerous other safer alternatives (see Meuninck 2013).

Traditional uses: *T. plicata* is a male warrior plant used by Native Americans in sweeping, smudging with smoke, and steam-bath rituals to clear the body and mind of evil spirits that prevent good health. Northwestern tribes make fine cedar boxes for cooking and storage. Europeans use the wood to line chests and encasements because of the fine fragrance and insect-repulsing chemistry of the

Red cedar on Vancouver Island

wood. A decoction of dried and powdered leaves used as an external analgesic to treat painful joints, sores, wounds, and injuries. Leaf infusion used to treat coughs and colds. The decoction of the bark in water was used to induce menstruation and possibly as an abortifacient. The leaf buds (new-end growth) chewed to treat lung ailments. A decoction of leaves and boughs used to treat arthritis.

Modern uses: *Thuja occidentalis* is preferred over *Thuja plicata* as a homeopathic drug to treat rheumatism, poor digestion, depression, and skin conditions. Because of its thujone content, this is a drug used only with professional consultation and supervision.

Notes: This magnificent tree, tall and thick, is a giant of old-growth forests in the Northwest—it makes a durable, decay-resistant wood. Cedar boxes are still used to steam salmon and other foods: Hot rocks are placed on wet plants (often skunk cabbage leaves are wrapped around salmon), and the cedar box is covered with a lid, then the salmon is slow-cooked over steam or pit-cooked surrounded by wet grass under a fire. The trunk of red cedar used to make totem poles and canoes. The inner bark used as basket making material.

SAGE, SAGEBRUSH

Asteraceae *(Artemisia tridentata* Nutt.*)*

Identification: Found on arid land, this gray, fragrant shrub grows to 7' tall. Leaves are wedged shaped, lobed (3 teeth), broad at tip, tapering to the base. Yellow and brownish flowers form spreading, long, narrow clusters—blooms from July to October. Seed is hairy achene.

Habitat: Dry areas of US West and Southwest.

Food: Seeds, raw or dried, are ground into flour and eaten as a survival food. Seeds added to liqueurs for fragrance and flavor.

Traditional uses: A powerful warrior plant used for smudging and sweeping to rid the victim of bad airs and evil spirits. Also used as a tea to treat infections and stomachaches or ease childbirth, or as a wash for sore eyes. Leaves are soaked in water and applied as a

Sage, Clark's Fork of Yellowstone

poultice over wounds. Limbs used as switches in sweat baths to stimulate circulation. The leaf infusion used to treat sore throats, coughs, colds, and bronchitis. A decoction or infusion used as a wash for sores, cuts, and pimples. The aromatic decoction from steaming the herb inhaled for respiratory ailments and headaches. The decoction taken internally to treat diarrhea and externally as an anti-rheumatic. Decoction is cathartic.

Modern uses: Still very popular and important in Native American Church rituals, including smudging, sweeping, in sweat lodge, and as a disinfectant. For details, see the DVD *Native American Medicine and Little Medicine* (Meuninick, Clark, and Roman 2007).

Notes: Add this herb to your hot bath, hot tub, or sweat lodge for a fragrant, disinfecting, and relaxing cleansing. It is often the only source of firewood in the desert.

SITKA VALERIAN

Valerianaceae *(Valeriana sitchensis* Bong.; *Valeriana officinalis* L.)

Identification: Perennial to 24", sometimes higher. Leaves opposite, staggered up the stem, often with several basal leaves. Terminal cluster of white to cream-colored odiferous flowers, petals are feathery. Blooms April to July.

Sitka valerian

Habitat: Montane plant, typically found on north-facing slopes and plentiful in alpine meadows and along trails in the Olympics, Cascades, North Cascades, Mount Rainier, and Mount Baker, especially along Heliotrope Trail toward the climber's route.

Food: Edible roots not worth the effort; if you have had the foul-smelling valerian tea, you are nodding your head.

Traditional uses: Stress-reducing, tension-relieving mild sedative for insomniacs. *V. sitchensis* roots are decocted in water to treat pain, colds, and diarrhea. A poultice of the root used to treat cuts, wounds, bruises, and inflammation.

Modern uses: A few practitioners use *V. sitchensis* in the traditional way. Aqueous extract of *V. officinalis* root in a double-blind study had significant effect on poor or irregular sleepers. Valerian combined with hops enhances the sedative effect. The effect of valerian on gamma amino butyric acid (GABA) may reduce blood pressure and help mild depression; this chemical (GABA) is also high in evening primrose seeds and several varieties of tomatoes (GR).

Notes: Take the road to the Sunrise Lodge on the north side of Mount Rainier, walk to the learning center garden, and see this plant and many other medicinal plants of the US West and Northwest—a splendid setting. The plant's odiferous flowers are not particularly pleasant to many, but I love that stink; it means I'm back in the mountains.

Pacific yew

YEW, AMERICAN YEW AND ENGLISH YEW
Rhamnaceae *(Taxus brevifolia Nutt.)*

Identification: *T. brevifolia* is an evergreen shrub to scanty small tree that grows to 50'. Bark is papery, reddish purple to red brown. Drooping branches. Flat leaves (needles) in opposite rows. Flowers are small cones. Scarlet fruit is berrylike, with fleshy cup around a single seed.

Habitat: From Northern California, Oregon, and Washington through Idaho and Montana, north to British Columbia and Alberta on foothills and moist, shady sites.

Food: According to Daniel Moerman (1998), the Karok and Mendocino ate the ripe red fruit, but the seed and all other parts of the plant are toxic. Unless guided by an expert, avoid eating any part of this plant.

Traditional uses: Native Americans used the wet needles of American yew (*T. brevifolia*) as a poultice over wounds. Natives considered needles a panacea, a powerful tonic; boiled and used over injuries to alleviate pain. Bark decoctions used to treat stomachache. Native Americans were the first to use this plant to treat cancer.

Modern uses: The toxic drug taxine (paclitaxel) from American yew is used to treat cancer. It prevents cell multiplication and may prove an effective therapy for leukemia and cancer of the cervix, ovaries, and breasts. Clinical trials continue with the drug.

Notes: Research reports that the cancer-fighting chemistry is in both species. It takes nearly 3,000 trees or 9,000 kg of dried inner bark of *T. brevifolia* to make 1 kg of the drug Taxol. Taxol today is grown in culture from cloned cells in huge bioreactor tanks. Researchers are attempting to produce the drug from pinene from pine trees.

CAUTION: Both species can induce abortion. All parts of the plant are toxic. Unless guided by an expert, avoid eating any part of this plant.

Chapter Two: Medicinal Plants of Forests East and West

Trees, shrubs, and soft-tissue plants provide a splendid pharmacopeia both East and West and have been used for millennia as food and medicine. Here are a few of my favorites.

Black Walnut (Juglans), 16

Bloodroot (Sanguinaria), 17

Ginseng (Panax), 17

Golden seal (Hydrastis), 19

Grapes (Vitis), 20

Hawthorn (Crataegus), 21

Mayapple (Podophyllum), 22

Oaks (Quercus), 23

Poplars (Populus), 24

Pawpaw (Asimina), 25

Slippery Elm (Ulmus), 26

Witch Hazel (Hamamelis), 27

Black walnut

BLACK WALNUT
Juglandaceae *(Juglans nigra L.)*
Identification: Large hardwood tree, bark ridged, deeply grooved, dark with large leaves, 7–17 leaflets, which are toothed, narrow, rough, and slightly hairy underneath. Break a hairless twig, and the pith is light brown and chambered. Flower is catkin forming in April or May. Fruit is 1"–2" in diameter, with a round husk over a nut meat inside.

Habitat: Found in eastern United States, in fertile soil, often lining roadsides where harvest of nut crop is easy in September and October.

Food: Nuts used in baked goods, cereals, waffles, pancakes, and salads. Eat them out of hand. A favorite recipe is black-walnut pawpaw-fruit chocolate cake: Simply use a standard chocolate cake mix and stir in 1 cup of pawpaw fruit; garnish chocolate frosting with black walnut meats.

Traditional uses: Native Americans used the bark, inner bark, leaves, and nut meats as food and medicine. The bark chewed to treat mouth sores and toothaches. Husks of nuts and the crushed leaves used to treat ringworm. The decoction of bark is emetic. An infusion of nutshells used as a wash over itchy inflammations. Oil from the nut used as a lotion and hair oil. Charred twigs, sticks, and bark applied to wounds, burns, and bites; the sap smoothed over bites and inflammations (see Moerman 1998).

Modern uses: Black walnut husk extract is antifungal; combine equal parts of tincture of goldenseal, cinnamon, tea tree oil, and black walnut husk tincture for an antifungal compound. Black walnuts as health food are little studied, but research from Loma Linda University (California) on English walnuts (California walnuts) demonstrated a positive cholesterol-reducing ability. Participants ate 20 percent of calories from walnuts, and their ratio of LDL to HDL lowered by 12 percent (http://ajcn.nutrition.org/content/59/5/995.abstract). Walnuts may help prevent hyperthyroidism and scabies and may lessen inflammation of psoriasis and arthritis because of their omega-3 content). Walnuts are rich in mood-enhancing serotonin, and they may improve satiety by reducing cravings, thereby treating obesity. Although juglone from walnut hull may be carcinogenic, walnut extracts are Commission E–approved externally for skin inflammations and excessive perspiration (see *PDR for Herbal Medicines* 2007, 882).

Notes: Many plants cannot grow in the toxic soil beneath a walnut tree. To remove the husk—the stain-producing covering of the walnut—put the walnuts on a paved driveway and roll them under your shoe, or jack up a car 1" off the ground, engage the transmission, and shoot the walnuts under the tire; see a simple electric walnut huller in action in my video *Trees, Shrubs, Nuts & Berries* (Meuninick and Duke 2007). Rocking-chair storytellers say walnut husk oil will dye your hair and may produce new hair growth.

BLOODROOT, RED PUCCOON, RED INDIAN PAINT

Papavaraceae *(Sanguinaria canadensis* L.)*

Identification: Perennial to 7" with a ⅜"-thick, slightly curved rhizome that exudes red liquid when cut; reddish rootlets. Leaves are down covered, grayish green, and clasping; they grow in a basal rosette, with 5–9 lobes, accented underneath with protruding ribs. Flower is single, white, with 8–12 petals; short-lived, early spring bloomer. Flower clasps leave as it blooms.

Habitat: Eastern forests south to Florida, west to Minnesota, and north to Manitoba.

Food: Toxic.

Traditional uses: Native Americans discovered that the herb induced vomiting. Pioneers and First Peoples used the root extraction to treat rheumatism, fevers, and laryngitis. Folk practitioners

Bloodroot

suggest a small dose works as an appetite stimulant, attributed to the bitter alkaloids that stimulate the digestive system reflexively. The root juice used to treat warts. It is anesthetic.

Modern uses: Research (in vitro) shows that sanguinarine and chelerythrine found in bloodroot have anticancer properties. Sanguinarine exhibits antimicrobial, tumoricidal, anticancer, antiangiogenic, and antimicrotubule properties. However, its efficacy has not been tested in humans. Still used topically as an anti-inflammatory. Sanguinarine, although toxic, has low oral toxicity and is antiseptic (*PDR for Herbal Medicines* 2007, 115)—used in a name-brand mouthwash and toothpaste.

Notes: There are reports that the red bloodroot exudate, when thinned with water and applied to the skin, is an effective mosquito repellent. In human tests, I have found this to be true. I use the root juice to ward off mosquitoes; see DVD *Native American Medicine and Little Medicine* (Meuninck, Clark, and Roman 2007).

GINSENG

Araliaceae *(Panax ginseng* C.A. Meyer; *P. quinquefolius* L.)*

Identification: Perennial to 3' in height. Stem smooth and round with 3–5 leaves in terminal whorls of 3–5 palmate leaflets. Leaflets finely serrated, 3"–8" long, 1"–2" wide. Greenish-yellow flowers give rise to a round, glossy, pea-size seed.

Panax quinquefolius

Dwarf ginseng, Panax trifolius

Habitat: Cultivated from coast to coast, found wild in the Northwest and eastern forested areas—rare, overharvested—needs shade, a forest with mature canopy, and well-drained soil.

Traditional uses: Native Americans used the root as a ceremonial fetish to frighten ghosts. Decoction made from fresh or dried roots reduced fever and induced sweating. The root considered a panacea in China and Korea as a tonic and adaptogen (helps user to adapt to stress). Ginseng root considered a stimulant and an aphrodisiac that enhances the immune response and may improve cerebral circulation and function as well as regulate blood pressure and blood sugar. In traditional Chinese medicine terms, it increases libido and is a tonic for the spleen and lungs.

Modern uses: *P. quinquefolius* proven effective against mixed anxiety-depressive disorder (MAD) (Chatterjee, Verma, and Palit 2010). Chinese, Russian, Korean, and European studies suggest that ginseng enhances production of interferon-improving phagocytosis. As an ergogenic aid it may improve endurance, potentiating normal function of the adrenal gland (GR). It also regulates plasma glucose. Other research suggests anti-cancer, anti-proliferative, and antitumor activity against leukemia and lymphoma. University of Chicago researchers treated two types of colorectal cancer cells with steamed American ginseng root extract, causing damage to the rogue cells' mitochondria, leading to apoptosis (cell death) (NIH). Ginseng has antimicrobial and antifungal activity. Cold-FX, an over-the-counter treatment for colds, contains ginseng; proven effective in clinical trials. Root preparations are immune-system stimulants that help to resist infection. Preliminary studies suggest extract may increase mental acuity and has an estrogen-like effect on women (*PDR for Herbal Medicine* 2007, 386). It may thwart radiation sickness and other physical, chemical, and biological stressors, thereby supporting its anti-stress applications (*PDR for Herbal Medicine* 2007, 387). Ginseng is considered by many the closest thing to a cure-all in nature.

Notes: Order ginseng, rare in the wild, at www.herbs.com. Many over-the-counter purchased Chinese herbs harbor eggs and larvae that later emerge as exotic flying insects and fast-moving beetles. Scrub these roots thoroughly before use.

CAUTION: Use this herb under the supervision of a professional health-care practitioner. Avoid during pregnancy and while nursing until further studies are available.

GOLDENSEAL
Ranunculaceae *(Hydrastis canadensis* **L.***)*

Goldenseal

Identification: Perennial to 11" in height with a bright yellow (golden) rhizome. Has 2 ribbed leaves; lower leaf is typically smaller, sessile; upper leaf has a long petiole with 7 lobes, finely serrated. Flower is solitary, found on an erect stem, with 3 small greenish-white petals that quickly disappear. Fruits are scarlet, with 1 or 2 glossy black seeds.

Habitat: Cultivated nationwide, the plant is native to eastern forests and prefers wet, well-drained soil. Produces spreading colonies on banks in woods; often found growing near ginseng.

Traditional uses: Air-dried rhizomes and root fibers ground and infused to treat diarrhea. Cherokee used root decoction as a cancer treatment and as a tonic and wash for inflammations, infections, and wounds. Goldenseal is as an appetite stimulant. The dried root chewed to treat whooping cough. A decoction used for earaches. An aqueous decoction of the root applied as eyewash. Root steeped in whisky taken as heart tonic. Tuberculosis, scrofula, liver problems, and gallbladder problems traditionally treated with the root extraction.

Modern uses: Standardized extracts from air-dried rhizomes and root hairs taken with water or in capsules to stimulate bile and hydrochloric-acid secretion to hasten and improve peristalsis. The drug has a weak antibiotic and weak antineoplastic (anticancer) activity in vitro. It may constrict peripheral blood vessels and is said to stimulate and cleanse the liver. Used as a therapy for upper respiratory infections (GR). Taken internally, goldenseal may increase depressed white blood cell counts, as reported in traditional Chinese medicine research. Clinical trials suggest its effectiveness against traveler's diarrhea. The root paste can be applied externally to treat wounds and fungal infections. Goldenseal's bitter taste stimulates hunger and may treat anorexia. The National Center for Complementary and Alternative Medicine (NCCAM) is funding research on goldenseal, including studies of antibacterial mechanisms and potential cholesterol-lowering effects. NCCAM is also funding development of research-grade goldenseal to facilitate clinical studies (NIH). Ethanol extract of goldenseal is antimicrobial.

Notes: Goldenseal is scarce in the wild due to overharvesting. Many botanical gardens exhibit goldenseal, and the plant is widely cultivated in the United States and Canada. I have used goldenseal for treating athlete's foot by mixing equal amounts of cinnamon, oregano, and goldenseal powder, moistening the mixture with alcohol, and then applying it with a cotton swab to areas of the foot and between the toes.

CAUTION: Do not take goldenseal if you are pregnant or lactating. Goldenseal is extremely bitter. It is nontoxic at recommended dosages.

Concord grapes escaped cultivation

GRAPES, WINE, AND GRAPESEED EXTRACT

Vitaceae *(Vitis vinifera* L.; *Vitis labrusca* L.)*

Identification: Hairless, scaly, climbing vine to 160'. Vine hangs free and does not cling with hairs to substrate. Yellowish-green flowers in tight panicle (cluster). Fruit has characteristics of grapes bought in a market but smaller, seedy.

Habitat: Nationwide, also indigenous to Europe and Asia. American wild varieties found in forests, along forest edges, and marshy areas looping through and vines hanging free (versus clinging) from trees.

Food: Fruit especially delicious when picked frozen in winter. Add this fruit to your daily diet. Eat organic when possible.

Traditional uses: *V. labrusca* (fox grape) fruit was used to treat diarrhea. The leaf infusion administered as blood-cleansing tonic. Wilted leaves applied as a poultice over sore breasts. Leaves also used to stop bleeding, inflammation, and pain, such as pain of hemorrhoids. Unripe grapes sucked and chewed to treat sore throats, and raisins used for constipation and thirst. The root decoction administered to treat rheumatism. An infusion of the shaggy bark used for urinary problems. A wet poultice treated headaches. Fruit consumed to reduce nausea and prevent vomiting.

Modern uses: Preliminary research suggests grapeseed extract may be effective as an antioxidant to treat pancreatitis and edema. The extract appears to improve blood flow (venous efficiency) and symptoms related to retinal pathology, including resistance to glare and poor vision in low light (this effect, however, effectiveness challenged by recent research). The seed extract may improve microcirculatory function (CM). It is a capillary protectant, an anti-inflammatory, and an antioxidant. Grapeseed extract used to treat heart patients and prevent artery damage. This feature is due to the protective activity of bioflavonoids. In Europe, extract used to treat varicose veins and other compromised capillary blood-flow problems due to platelet aggregation, diabetes, and altered blood rheology. Preliminary studies suggest grapeseed extract may induce hair growth. Follow recommended dosages on the package. Evidence from one trial suggests that grapeseed extract (50 mg daily) may improve vision in low light. Grapeseed extract treats a wide range of diseases related to oxidative damage. Several double-blind placebo-controlled, crossover trials highlighted in various journals show this antioxidant effect (NIH) (see *PDR for Herbal Medicines* 2007, 407).

The phenolic compounds found in grapes—especially dark-skinned grapes (including wild grapes)—may improve heart function and mental function and protect against heart disease and Alzheimer's. Ayurvedic medicine advocates eating raisins for chronic bronchitis, heart disease, gout, fevers, and enlarged spleen or liver. Unsweetened grape juice treats constipation, especially in children. Studies show red wine raises HDL, providing a protective effect and reducing the risk of developing coronary heart disease.

Notes: To make a tart marmalade, pick and blend the grapes and then simmer to thicken. Do not add sugar. This produces a freezer jam that is rich in bioflavonoids. Grapes leaves are edible and may be steamed and wrapped around rice dishes. Eat grapes raw, lightly cooked, or fermented. The unfermented juice may not be as effective as wine for antioxidants, capillary protectant, and anti-inflammatory actions. Tannins and other phenolic compounds released from skins provide a more potent mix of protection when released during fermentation.

CAUTION: Poison ivy vines cling from hairs and do not hang free—know the difference. Moonseed looks grapelike but is poisonous (see Meuninck 2014). Do not take wine and other alcoholic beverages during pregnancy or while nursing.

HAWTHORN

Rosaceae (*Crataegus* spp.; *C. laevigata* (Poiret) D.C.; *C. monogyna* Jacquin Emend; *C. oxyacantha*; *C. douglasii* Lindl; *C. macrosperma* Ashe)

Identification: Shrubs to small trees 6′–20′ in height, many branched, branches thorny. Yellow-green glossy leaves, 3–5 lobed, with lobes forward-pointing and serrated leaf edges. Numerous white flowers are in terminal clus-

Hawthorn

ters, with 10–20 stamens that give rise to small apple-like fruit. Fruit ovoid to round, red or black, mealy. There is 1 seed in each chamber of the ovary.

Habitat: Hawthorn species thrive nationwide except in extreme cold and heat. Seek the trees in wet woods and edges of woodlots. *C. macrosperma* is found in the United States east of the prairie.

Food: The mealy and seedy fruit is eaten out of hand, but its heart-protecting value makes it worth the trouble. Fruit may be sliced, dried, and decocted, or infused in water to make a health-protecting drink. It blends tastefully with green tea. Berries are gathered in August; immerse in boiling water for 30 seconds, then cut in half, remove and discard seeds, and dry berries in a food dryer.

Traditional uses: Hawthorn has long been a treatment for congestive heart disease in Europe and China. The active phytochemistry includes bioflavonoids that improve peripheral circulation to the heart and the extremities, including the brain. They also improve coronary blood flow and are hypotensive. Native Americans chewed the leaves and applied the masticated mash to sores and wounds as a poultice. Shoots were used in infusion to treat children's diarrhea. Thorns were thrashed on arthritic joints as a counterirritant. The Okanagan-Colville Nation's herbal art included burning the thorn down to the skin, not totally unlike incense burning (moxibustion) on Chinese acupuncture needles to heighten effect. A decoction of new shoots was used to wash mouth sores. Numerous other remedies are covered in Daniel Moerman's *Native American Ethnobotany* (1998).

Modern uses: Commission E–approved for skin inflammations. Most studies have used *C. laevigata* leaves, fruit, blossoms, and new-end growth, which is said to improve and protect cardiac and vascular function by dilating coronary blood vessels and initiating heart muscle regeneration. Extract may be anti-angina and improve Buerger's disease (paresthesia of the foot or toe, an arterial spasm) (NIH). Also used to treat tachycardia. Considered cholesterol lowering and hypotensive (GR). The plant's anthocyanidins and proanthocyanidin are synergistic with vitamin C. In European studies, standardized extract improved exercise tolerance in heart patients. Other studies suggest that the extract may alleviate leg pain caused by partially occluded coronary arteries (CM). Chinese practitioners decoct the dried fruit and use it for treating irritable bowel and gallbladder problems. The berry is considered antibacterial to shigella (dysentery) species.

Notes: Herbs with circulation-stimulating properties in addition to hawthorn include garlic, ginger, *Ginkgo biloba* extract, and cayenne. My brother grows about a dozen hawthorn trees that have the biggest, sweetest fruit I have ever tasted. In spring, we cut off a few dozen clusters of flower buds and emerging new-growth leaves to make a tea. The hot water extracts the bitter bioflavonoids that are hypotensive and anti-angina. I have decocted fresh flower tops and experienced flushing and lightheadedness. Perhaps the decoction was too concentrated. I definitely felt enhanced peripheral circulation in the form of face flushing.

CAUTION: Not recommended during pregnancy and lactation.

MAYAPPLE, AMERICAN MANDRAKE

Berberidaceae (*Podophyllum peltatum* L.)

Identification: Woodland perennial with umbrella-like leaves, 2 cleft leaves on a single, stout stalk, each leaf with 5–7 lobes. Single white flower is tucked under leaves; petiole is attached in axil of leaves. Fruit ripens from mid- to late summer; edible only when ripe. Plant colonies spread over the forest floor.

Habitat: Rich woods in dense to slightly open eastern forests.

Food: The fruit is eaten in summer when soft and ripe. Many plants die off in summer; the plants do not always provide abundant fruit and are relished by forest creatures. Cook the fruit or, if it is completely ripe, eat it out of hand. Native Americans smashed and dried the fruit into fruit cakes to later reconstitute in water and use as a sauce.

Traditional uses: Minute doses of mayapple were used by Native Americans to treat a variety of illnesses including verrucae (wart produced by papillomavirus). It is an emetic and purgative—a powerful laxative. ***Warning:*** The root is toxic and may kill worm infestations, but beware; the constituents are toxic internally—professional practitioners only. Root powder applied externally on difficult-to-heal sores. Fresh juice from the root (approximately 1 drop) put in the ear to improve hearing. In the mid-twentieth century, mayapple resin injected into venereal warts as a treatment.

Modern uses: *P. peltatum* is Commission E–approved for treating warts, specifically genital warts. The root extract contains an antimitotic agent that led to the formulation of synthetic etoposide, a treatment for small-cell lung cancer and testicular cancer (GR).

Notes: Mayapple appears about the same time as morels. I prepare mayapple root water as a garden insecticide. Blend about 8 ounces of fresh root in 2 quarts of water, then strain the mixture through cheesecloth or panty hose into a garden sprayer. (For details see the DVD *Native American Medicine and Little Medicine* [Meuninick, Clark, and Roman 2007]).

Mayapple

CAUTION: The roots and leaves are poisonous, and handling the roots may cause allergic dermatitis. Avoid using the plant as a drug without medical supervision. Drug may be absorbed through the skin—an allergen, toxic, and antimitotic.

OAKS

Fagaceae *(Quercus* spp.)

Identification: Visit an arboretum with labeled oak trees to assist identification. Armed with visual proof, you will be more successful in the bush gathering nuts for the winter. Oaks typically have rounded leaf lobes or pointed leaf lobes. Oaks with pointed leaf ends typically have the most bitter nut meats. White oak when mature has gray to whitish bark; red and black oak have black bark.

White oak

Habitat: Various species found nationwide in yards, woodlots, forested areas, and roadsides.

Food: As mentioned, acorns from oaks with rounded leaf lobes are less bitter than acorns from species of oaks with pointed leaf lobes. White oak (*Q. alba*), bur oak (*Q. macrocarpa*), swamp chestnut oak (*Q. michauxii*), and chestnut oak (*Q. prinus*) are good examples of sweet acorns from the eastern United States. The chinquapin oak or yellow chestnut oak (*Q. muehlenbergii*) has bittersweet acorns. Out west, look for Gambel oak (*Q. gambelii*), blue oak (*Q. douglasii*), and Oregon white oak (*Q. garryana*) for sweeter meats. Tannins in acorns embitter the taste, but water-soluble tannins leach away in water. A quick fix in the kitchen is to puree acorn meat in a blender, using 2 cups of water for every cup of nut meat. Blend thoroughly, strain, and press the water out of the nut meat.

Traditional uses: White oak, *Q. alba*, has tannin-rich bark. Tannins are antiseptic and astringent. Native Americans and pioneers made a tea from the bark for mouth sores, burns, cuts, and scrapes. The bark extraction, considered a panacea, believed to provide cancer protection. Dried and powdered bark sprinkled over the navel of an infant to heal the wound caused by removing the umbilical cord.

Modern uses: Oak bark extract, typically from *Q. robur* (English oak) or *Q. petraea*, is Commission E–approved for treating bronchitis, cough, diarrhea, mouth and throat sores, and inflammations of the skin. Chemicals from oak bark are being tested as a cancer therapy.

Notes: Tannins have antioxidant properties that protect cells from oxidative damage. Tannins inhibit superoxide radicals and inhibit growth of many fungi, yeasts, bacteria, and viruses. Tannins accelerate blood clotting, reduce blood pressure, decrease the serum lipid level, produce liver necrosis, and are somewhat immuno-suppressing (Chung et al. 1998).

Balsam producing end growth

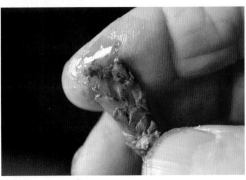

Balsam resin exuding

POPLARS: BALSAM POPLAR, ASPEN, COTTONWOOD

Salicaceae *(Populus balsamifera* L.; *P. tremuloides* **Michx.;** *P. deltoides* **Bartr. ex Marsh***)*

Identification: Many poplars have ovate leaves on long petioles that provide the quaking effect when the wind blows. Flowers are drooping catkins. Cottonwood *(P. deltoides)* has thick furrowed bark when mature. Aspen *(P. tremuloides)* is distinctive with its greenish-white bark and quaking leaves. Balsam poplar *(P. balsamifera)* has broad heart-shaped leaves, 6"–10", edged with fine teeth; slightly flattened to rounded leaf stalks. New-growth end buds of balsams are sticky (resinous) and aromatic. The young balsam poplar's bark is gray green and smooth; the mature tree has dark, grooved bark.

Habitat: Widely distributed in United States. Requires ample water. Balsam poplar is found in the northern tier of states and throughout southern and central Canada. Cottonwoods reside typically in low, wet areas nationwide. Locate aspens in stands on mountain slopes, in mountain meadows, and along rivers.

Food: Balsam poplar cambium (the inner bark) is eaten raw or boiled, dried, and pounded to flour, and then mixed with corn flour (masa) and or wheat flour to make bread. Simmer shoots and leaf buds and catkins in water—fair tasting. The vitamin C content is high.

Traditional uses: Native Americans considered balsam poplar a panacea: The inner bark decoction was used as a tonic, a treatment for colds, and a system cleanser after acute infections. The bark maceration and decoction was used as a wash for rheumatism. Pioneers gathered the reddish resin covering new growth and thinned the resin in an alcohol solvent. The resulting salve was applied to seal and heal wounds and relieve inflammations.

Modern uses: Bark, leaves, and leaf buds used in modern therapies. Leaf-bud extract is healing, antibacterial, and antiphlogistic (relieves inflammation); it is Commission E–approved to treat hemorrhoids, wounds, and burns. Salicin from the bark and leaves is analgesic (a precursor of aspirin) (GR). The bark and leaves are antispasmodic and used to treat arthritis, rheumatism, and pain and urinary complaints due to prostate hypertrophy. The bitter tonic effect and alterative effect may make it helpful in treating anorexia (GR).

Notes: Avoid use if you are allergic to aspirin or other salicylates. Tapped poplar trees produce sap; sugar content is low, and too much boiling is required to sweeten the brew.

PAWPAW, PAPAW

Anonaceae (*Asimina triloba* L. Dunal.)

Identification: Small, delicate, shade-loving tree. Leaves large, 8"–12", toothless, lance shaped, broadening toward the tip, terminating in a point; darker green above, lighter green underneath. Striking red flowers with 6 petals precede leaves, and (if pollinated) develop gradually into 3"–6" fruits. Fruit banana to mango shaped, soft and dark brown when ripe.

Pawpaw fruit

Habitat: Texas east to Florida and north to Iowa, Illinois, Michigan, and New Jersey—understory in mature forests.

Food: Fall fruit eaten fresh. Unripe fruit will ripen in a few days or a couple of weeks, but when ripe the soft, fresh fruit will keep only a couple of days in the refrigerator. The flavor is sweet, intense, and mango-like—loved by many, disdained by a few. Blend the fruit with ice cream into milk shakes.

Pawpaw flower

Traditional uses: Cherokees and Iroquois ate the fruit smashed and dried into small cakes for winter use. When reconstituted the dried fruit was blended into corn masa to make corn bread. The inner bark used to make cordage. Medicinal uses are undocumented.

Modern uses: Research at Purdue University may yield a potent anticancer chemical from the leaves and stems of the plant. These pawpaw-derived compounds help cut the amount of energy going to high-energy cells such as cancer cells. Studies suggest pawpaw acetogenins support the body's cells during times of stress. Pawpaw extract appears to modulate cellular energy, modulate blood vessel growth, and inhibit cell division (Coothankandaswamy et al. 2010).

Notes: Pawpaw trees are protogynous: The stigma of the flower ripens before the pollen; thus the trees cannot self-pollinate. In the fall, shake and pound the trees to fell the fruit. Pawpaws grow under the sheltering canopy of mature maples and beech trees, protected from direct sunlight; if storms blow down sheltering trees, the pawpaws burn alive.

SLIPPERY ELM, RED ELM
Ulmaceae *(Ulmus rubra* Muhl.*)*

Slippery elm leaf and twig

Identification: Deciduous grows to 70′ in height with spreading branches and open crown. Older bark is rough and fissured; young branches are reddish brown and downy. Leaf buds are large and downy. Leaves are obovate to oblong, darker green on top, rough to the touch, with a double serrated toothed margin; to 8″, typically shorter. Flowers, with up to 9 sepals and stamens, grow in dense, sessile clusters. Spinning-top-shaped fruit grows to 1″ long.

Habitat: North America, typically east of the Missouri River, in forests and fields

Food: Not edible.

Traditional uses: The inner bark used in infusion to treat gastritis and ulcers. The bark extract from this tree acts as an antioxidant and, because it is mucilaginous and demulcent, as an emollient. Externally, the aqueous extract is an excellent wound dressing. Applied to burns; also used to treat gout, rheumatism, and arthritis. The outer bark used to induce abortions.

Modern uses: Slippery elm used by holistic-medicine practitioners to treat colds, sore throats, and bronchitis. The outer bark used to make salve. The inner bark is dried and powdered, then added to water and drunk for gastric ulcers, duodenal ulcers, and colitis (GR). The bark fraction used in the Essiac cancer remedy, an unproven combination of slippery elm bark, sheep sorrel, burdock root, and turkey rhubarb root (NIH). Purchase these compounds as lozenges, powder, or cut and sifted. Use the product for making tea and as a demulcent for respiratory irritations. See your licensed professional holistic health-care practitioner for consultation. Powdered bark is mixed with water to create a paste applied to wounds (*PDR of Herbal Medicines* 2007, 755).

Note: Add this attractive tree to the garden for its beauty and timeless medicinal qualities.

WITCH HAZEL

Hamamelidaceae *(Hamamelis virginiana* L.*)*

Witch hazel

Identification: Deciduous small bushy tree or shrub. Grows to 10′ in height and occasionally much taller. Bark is thin, brown on the outside, red on the inside. Younger branches are hairy and yellow brown. Leaves alternate, blunt, indented, with rough margins. Before leaves emerge, 5–7 yellow, short-stemmed flowers appear in clusters. Flowers grow from the axils of leaf buds. Petals are bright, long, narrow, linear, and roll to a spiral in the bud. Fruit capsule is oddly shaped, woody, oval, about ¾″ long.

Habitat: Typically east of the Mississippi River and in coastal forests. I have found it growing in Michigan in the forested dunes area of Warren Dunes and Grand Mere.

Food: Not edible.

Traditional uses: Witch hazel used by Cherokee, Chippewa, Iroquois, Mohegan, Menominee, and Potawatomi, all living in the entire range of the plant east of the Mississippi. They used the leaf tea externally to treat muscle aches, athlete's food, wounds, burns, and various skin afflictions. Tea consumed for coughs, asthma, colds, sore throats, dysentery, and diarrhea. Twigs and inner bark still used in infusion to treat colds, pain, sores, fevers, sore throat, and tuberculosis. An infusion of twigs used to treat dysentery and diarrhea. Decoction of new-growth tips and shoots, from the base of the plant, used as a blood purifier or spring tonic. Native Americans and pioneers used young-end tips in decoction to treat colds and coughs. Root and twig decoctions considered a cure-all for just about any ailment: bruises, edema, cholera, and arthritis.

Modern uses: Distilled witch hazel water contains no tannins but is still astringent and used as a gargle for sore throat and sore gums and is Commission E–approved for external use on hemorrhoids, skin inflammations, varicose veins, wounds, burns, and for mouth and pharynx treatment. Commercial products include liniments, eye ointments, and skin-toning astringents. Witch hazel water is distilled from the leaves and twigs and used as an eyewash and to treat hemorrhoids, varicose veins, sore muscles, bruises, and sprains (CM). Tannins derived from distilling the active compound used to treat local skin irritations and inflammations, including eczema (GR).

Notes: Witch hazel is grown in nurseries, gardens, and arboretums and is an integral part of an effective wash I blend for psoriasis called Pharmaclean; for more information look under witch hazel at www.herbvideos.com.

Chapter Three: Medicinal Plants of Wetlands

This section covers medicinal plants found in wetlands of the eastern and western United States—plants used as medicine for centuries found in low-lying areas, such as marshes, bogs, rivers, lakes, streams, and fens.

Bittersweet Nightshade (Solanum), 30

Blueberry (Vaccinium), 30

Boneset (Eupatoria), 31

Club Moss (Huperzia), 32

Cranberry (Vaccinium), 33

Duckweed (Lemna), 34

Horsetail (Equisetum), 35

Elder (Sambucus), 36

Jewelweed (Impatiens), 37

Lobelia (Lobelia), 38

Mint (Mentha), 39

Paper Birch (Betula), 40

Sweet Flag (Acorus), 41

Tamarack (Larix), 42

Watercress (Nasturtium), 43

Willows (Salix), 44

BITTERSWEET NIGHTSHADE, CLIMBING NIGHTSHADE

Solanaceae (*Solanum dulcamara* L.)

Bittersweet nightshade

Identification: Climbing vine with dark, long leaves on short petioles, lobed, alternate. Purple, rocket-shaped flowers form in summer. Fruit is ¼"–½", round, reddish orange, and appears in fall. This is a member of the potato and tomato family.

Habitat: Found nationwide along streams, ditches, thickets, lakeshores, and bogs. Often clings to willow and other shrubs and hangs over the water.

Food: Not edible. Berries toxic.

Traditional uses: Root infusion administered by Native Americans to treat nausea and mixed with an unspecified herb to treat gas; also taken as an antiemetic. Its external use documented in the form of an oil-based salve. Plant long considered an anticancer drug (unproven).

Modern uses: Commission E–approved for treating warts, acne, eczema, and furuncles. Holistic practitioners have used the herb infusion for arthritis, gout, and respiratory problems, including bronchitis and coughing (GR).

Notes: Gather the herb in the fall of the year. It makes an attractive seasonal decoration, albeit one that should be kept away from young children who might eat the toxic berries.

CAUTION: Seek professional consultation and oversight when considering this herb. In vitro research suggests the herb has anticancer chemistry. Nightshade is toxic, although it is rarely fatal. I have never tried the herb and therefore cannot recommend it. Definitely do not take during pregnancy or while nursing.

BLUEBERRY, BILBERRY

Ericaceae (*Vaccinium myrtillus* L.)

Identification: Deciduous shrub with sharp-edged green branches that grows to 70" in height; wild types typically smaller. Leaves are alternate, ovate and oblong, finely serrated. Flowers greenish tinged with pink, ¼" long, containing 8–10 stamens that are shorter than the styles. Globular fruit are blue black, often frosted, with numerous small seeds dispersed through the purple pulp. Numerous species vary significantly. The terms *blueberry* and *bilberry* are used interchangeably.

Habitat: Northern tier states from coast to coast in wetlands, lowlands, and highlands, including eastern and western mountains.

Food: Fruit eaten fresh or dried. Leaves made into tea.

Traditional uses: Native Americans used a decoction of fresh or dried berries to treat diarrhea. The Iroquois used a whole aerial part decoction as a topical application to dermatitis. Bog blueberry *(V. uliginosum* L.*)* leaves infused in water and sugar and taken as a tonic by mother after childbirth. Blueberries are a good source of vitamin C and a folk use to prevent scurvy. Pulverized dried leaves infused and taken for nausea. Other Native American uses found in Moerman's *Native American Ethnobotany* (1998). Pioneers used the leaves in decoctions for treating diabetes. Berry tea taken to treat mouth sores and inflammations.

Blueberries

Modern uses: The use of fresh and dried fruits and dried leaves is Commission E–approved for treating diarrhea and inflammation of the pharynx and mouth. The fruit is an antioxidant and a capillary protectant that may improve blood flow to the feet, brain, hands, eyes, and other distal areas. It is antiplatelet aggregating, anti-glaucoma, and may provide protection from night blindness. Research suggests it may prevent varicose veins. Blueberry has induced the release of dopamine and may be helpful as adjunct nutritional support for Alzheimer's disease. A nutritionist at the University of Maine found evidence that wild blueberries, when eaten regularly in high volumes, may help improve or prevent pathologies associated with metabolic syndrome, including diabetes and heart disease (Vendrame 2014).

Notes: Eat a fistful of blueberries daily when experiencing bowel discomfort, gas, or diarrhea. Dry berries in a food dryer and store them in the freezer to treat winter stomach problems, or freeze them fresh.

BONESET, THOROUGHWORT
Asteraceae *(Eupatorium perfoliatum* L.*)*

Identification: This perennial grows to 5'. Plant rises from a hairy horizontal rootstock. Stems and leaves are hairy, rough. Leaves opposite, to 7" in length, lance shaped, tapering to a point, fused around the stem at the base. Stem appears to grow through the leaf. White flowers are florets that form large convex head at the top of the plant. Fruit is tufted.

Boneset

Habitat: Eastern United States in thickets and wetlands, open wet prairies, and marshes.

Food: Not edible.

Traditional uses: The leaf tea was considered an excellent nineteenth-century remedy to break fevers associated with acute infections; immune stimulating and used to treat colds, influenza, malaria, arthritis, painful joints, pneumonia, and gout, and to induce sweating. Whole aerial parts of plant applied as a poultice to relieve edema, swellings, and tumors. A Native American cure-all, it was used as a poultice over bone breaks to help set bones. Taken internally, the infusion of the aerial parts was cathartic and emetic. The infusion was used as a gargle to treat sore throat. Other uses included treating hemorrhoids, stomach pain, and headache; reducing chills; and alleviating urinary problems. (More uses are discussed in the CD-ROM *Herbal Odyssey* [Meunick 2007].)

Modern uses: Homeopaths use a microdose (homeopathic preparation) to treat colds, flu, and other febrile conditions (*PDR for Herbal Medicines* 2007, 121). When infused, the dried and commuted aerial parts of the herb are an immunostimulant taken to fight colds, flu, and other acute infections (GR).

Note: A striking, white flower head makes this plant worth adding to your garden. It provides late-season beauty.

CAUTION: Small doses of the herb are laxative and diuretic, whereas larger doses may induce catharsis and vomiting. Pyrrolizidine alkaloids present in this plant make it potentially dangerous to consume in any form, as these alkaloids have a liver-destroying capacity. Never use boneset without the consultation of a licensed holistic health-care practitioner.

Huperzia

CLUB MOSS, HUPERZIA
Lycopodiaceae *(Huperzia lucidula* (Michx) *Trevisan; H. selago* L.*)*

Identification: Low-lying, miniature-pine-like undergrowth to 10" tall. Found in colonies under hardwoods and conifers. Evergreen leaves are linear to lance shaped. Stems are forking and vegetative (producing embryonic shoots), with spores borne in a kidney-shaped sporangia on the stems at the bases of unmodified leaves.

Habitat: Found worldwide in moist areas under trees; probably originated in Eastern Europe and China.

Food: Not edible.

Traditional uses: Used by Native Americans as blood purifier, cold remedy, and dermatological aid. Traditional uses by Iroquois suggest immune-stimulating therapy against acute infections. *H. selago* is cathartic, purgative, emetic, and believed to strengthen immune function during woman's menses. Traditional use for headache, applied over eyes as a poultice.

Modern uses: Possible immune-stimulating herb. Of interest today for reported antiviral chemistry. Speculation suggests that it may be helpful against HIV infections. Has a diuretic effect when taken as an infusion. Homeopathic uses include treating liver and gallbladder problems, blood poisoning, respiratory inflammations, and inflammation of the female genitals (*PDR for Herbal Medicines* 2007, 206). Scientists have isolated a fungus from *H. serrata*, a Chinese species of *Huperzia,* that produces Huperzine A (HupA), a potentially better, less-toxic therapy for Alzheimer's and other neurologically degenerative diseases. HupA may also be effective against cardiovascular disease and cancer (Zhu et al. 2010).

Note: Huperzia is frequently found in forests in southwestern Michigan, typically when bushwhacking—a stunning find.

CRANBERRY

Ericaceae *(Vaccinium oxycossus* L.*)*
Identification: *Vaccinium oxycossus* is a low-lying evergreen dwarf shrub growing 5"–15" in height, creeping through bogs on slender stems; bark is hairy to smooth, brown to black in color. Flowers are pink; solitary or in couplets, rarely 3; nodding, with petals sharply bent backward like shooting stars. Fruit color ranges from pink to red, depending on ripeness. Small berries are juicy and tart.

Cranberry

Habitat: Found nationwide in the upper tier of states, covering the floor of sphagnum bogs, in hummocks and wet alpine meadows to elevations of 6,000'–7,000".

Food: You've tried cranberries with turkey, now try them in your favorite apple crisp recipe—add black walnuts and invite me over. Cranberries also spark up persimmon pudding and breakfast cereals.

Traditional uses: The berries and berry juice used as therapy for urinary tract infections—reported to acidify urine. Some claims that cranberry helps remove kidney stones. The juice also used to treat bladder infections and to prevent recurrence of urinary stones. It contains vitamin C and prevents scurvy.

Modern uses: Study showed drinking the juice may prevent adhesion of *Escherichia coli* to the linings of the gut, bladder, and urinary tract, thus preventing the bacterium from multiplying and inducing disease. In another study 16 ounces of cranberry juice was 73 percent effective against urinary tract infections. Cranberry juice also functions as a urine acidifier. Cranberries and cranberry juice decrease the odor and degradation of urine in incontinent patients. In one small study, 305 g of cooked cranberries proved effective in decreasing pH from 6.4 to 5.3; in other tests as much as 4 L of juice showed little effect on pH (NIH). However, there is evidence that using the juice with antibiotics may help suppress urinary tract infections. Personally, I have taken 1 ounce of the 100 percent extract in 6 ounces of dilution and effectively relieved a urinary tract infection. Of course, this may or may not work for you. Dosage of cranberries or cranberry extract to treat bladder infections and stones not established. Seek consultation from your holistic health-care professional (see Meuninck 2013).

Notes: In October, dry the ripe berries in a food dryer or cook them fresh. The popular over-the-counter cranberry cocktail juice contains too much sugar. It is prudent to take cranberry extract in pill form or buy pure 100 percent cranberry juice concentrate and sweeten it very little.

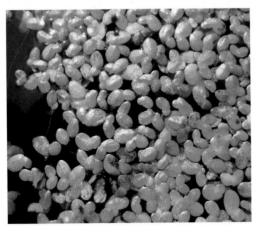
Lemna *species*

DUCKWEED
Lemnaceae *(Lemna minor* L.; *L. gibba;* and others)*

Identification: A hydroponic plant; one of the smallest flowering plants, spreading a green floating cover over stagnant ponds, marshes, and swamps. Its matching leaves look like Mickey Mouse ears. Threadlike root hairs pull water and minerals from pond. A green pond cover that looks scumlike from a distance.

Habitat: Found nationwide in ponds, still water, and marshes.

Food: The plant can be dried and made into tea. Add the fresh or dried duckweed to soups or blend it into cream soups. Always cook this plant, as its water source may be contaminated. It is virtually tasteless and tough, and small snails and other invertebrates are enmeshed in the tangle of plants. Clean away vermin and use sparingly.

Traditional uses: In China, the whole fresh plant used as a warming agent to treat hypothermia, flatulence, acute kidney infections, inflammation of upper respiratory tract, rheumatism, and jaundice. The whole plant is dried and powdered and used in infusion or decoction. The Iroquois used star duckweed, *L. trisulca,* as a poultice.

Modern uses: Homeopathically *L. minor* treats colds, fever, and upper respiratory tract infections (*PDR for Herbal Medicine* 2007, 264). Chinese traditional medicine uses the plant to treat acne, epilepsy, edema (swelling), and joint pain in combination with other herbs or with acupuncture as an adjunct therapy (Meuninck 2005). Duckweed is used to treat swelling (inflammation) of the upper airways and yellowing of skin due to liver problems and related jaundice. Also considered as a therapy for arthritis (unproven).

Notes: While working in Japan, I watched *Lemna* farmers motor over a pond with a long-shafted outboard boat that had a boxed screen surrounding the propeller. With the prop tilted toward the surface, duckweed was blasted against the screen. When clogged, the screen was placed in the sun to dry. The dried sheets of duckweed harvest used as food, animal forage, and medicine. Duckweed produces more protein per square meter than soybeans and is used to feed fish, shrimp, poultry, and cattle. Its ability to clean water by purifying and concentrating nutrients makes it a candidate for use on sewage ponds.

HORSETAIL, SCOURING RUSH, EQUISETUM

Equisetaceae *(Equisetum hyemale L.; E. arvense L.)*

Identification: A 3'–5' plant that appears in the spring as a naked segmented stem with a dry-tipped sporangium you can shake spores from. Later the sterile-stage stem arises with many long needlelike branches arranged in whorls up the stem. Silica rich, this stiff leafless plant spreads in colonies. Segmented parts of stem are pulled apart and put back together at the joints to make necklaces and bracelets.

Habitat: Found nationwide at edges of marshes, fens, bogs, streams, lakes, streams, and rivers.

Food: Native Americans of the Northwest eat the tender young shoots of the plant as a blood purifier (tonic). The tips (the strobili) boiled and eaten in Japan; mix them with rice wine vinegar, gin-

Equisetum

ger, and soy sauce, and enjoy. Native Americans of the Southwest eat the roots.

Traditional uses: Mexican Americans used the dried aerial plant parts of horsetail in infusion or decoction to treat painful urination. Equisetonin and bioflavonoids in the plant may account for its diuretic effect. Native Americans used a poultice of the stem to treat rashes of the armpit and groin. The Blackfoot used an infusion of the stem as a diuretic. Cherokees used the aerial part infusion to treat coughs in their horses. An infusion of the plant was used to treat dropsy, backaches, cuts, and sores. Baths of the herb were reported to treat syphilis and gonorrhea. This is one of the First Peoples' most widely used herbs.

Modern uses: Commission E–approved externally for wounds and burns and internally for urinary tract infections and kidney and bladder stones. Available over the counter (for dosages see *PDR for Herbal Medicines* 2007, 469).

Notes: This fast-spreading garden plant does well in the shade or sun and makes an interesting addition to a flower arrangement. When camping use the stems to clean pots and pans; the stem is silica rich.

CAUTION: An overdose of the herb may be toxic. Use only under the supervision of a skilled holistic health-care professional.

Sambucus canadensis

ELDER, ELDERBERRY

Adoxaceae *(Sambucus canadensis* L.; *S. racemosa* L.; *S. cerulean* Raf.; *Sambucus nigra* (L.) *R. Bolli.)*

Identification: All 3 species are clump-forming shrubs. *S. nigra* (an introduced European variety and the most studied) and our native eastern variety, *S. canadensis*, are very similar. These 2 varieties grow to 25' in height. Bark is light brown to gray, fissured, and flaky. Branches are green with gray lenticels; and they are easily broken at the conjunction petiole and stem. Leaves compound, leaflets oblong, ovate, serrated; matte green above, light bluish green underneath. White flowers in large, rounded, flat clusters. Fruit is oval, black to deep violet.

Habitat: Numerous species nationwide, typically in wet areas, along streams in lowlands and mountains of the East and West. *S. canadensis* is typically found in wet thickets, along edges of streams, rivers, and lakes in the eastern states and southeastern Canada. Purchase *S. nigra* from nurseries and transplant to your property.

Food: Use elder flowers and berries sparingly as food because their safety is not universally established; all berries were used to make beverages by native people—taste at your own risk. Dip the white cluster of blossoms in tempura batter and then cook them like fritters. Sprinkle with confectioners' sugar and serve as a health-protecting, heart-stimulating dessert. Or cook elderberries, then strain the juice through a sieve, thicken with pectin, and combine with other berry jams and marmalades. Add the cooked juice to maple syrup. The juice mixed with brown sugar, ginger, mustard, and soy makes a flavorful wonton dip. (Numerous recipes for this and other edible plants can be found in *Basic Illustrated Edible Wild Plants and Useful Herbs* [Meuninck 2013]).

Traditional uses: Flower infusions said to lower fever. A wash of the flowers may reduce fever and is soothing to irritations—considered anti-inflammatory, alterative, and diuretic. Flowers and fruit infused for influenza, flu, colds, arthritis, asthma, bronchitis, improving heart function, fevers, hay fever, allergies, and sinusitis. Native Americans scraped the bark and used the root in infusion as an emetic and a laxative. The berry infusion used to treat rheumatism. The flower infusion said to relieve colicky babies. Roots pounded, decocted, and applied to swollen breasts. Leaves in infusion used as a wash for sores.

Modern uses: Standardized extractions of *S. nigra* are Commission E–approved for treating cough, bronchitis, fevers, and colds. The therapeutic dose of flowers is reported to be 1–3 teaspoons of dried elder flowers to 1 cup off-the-boil water. Over-the-counter elderberry extracts indicate the recommended dosage on the bottle. Flower and berry extractions used to treat acute infections like colds and flu. Herbalist Michael Moore claims a tincture of the flowers is alterative and diaphoretic, stimulating the body's defense systems. Elderberry flower tinctures may be more effective and more tasteful when combined with mints. The berries can act like a mild laxative, yet at the same time are antidiarrheal and astringent. Current research suggests American elder leaf extract might work as a laxative, diuretic, and germ killer. American elder also contains lots of vitamin C (GR).

Notes: Cook then dry elder berries (fruit) in a food dryer, and then freeze for added protection and use judiciously in cooking throughout the cold months for disease prevention. Add dried berries of *S. canadensis* throughout the winter to cereal, pancakes, waffles, porridge, and in stir-fries. Berries are best when cooked again (reconstituted) in water or broth after drying. Flowers gathered in June are dried and made into tea. Be sure to cut away the stems before eating the flowers, and remove the stems from berries, too. Many cordials and syrup made from black elder flowers.

CAUTION: The leaves, bark, root, seeds, and unripe berries of *Sambucus* species may cause cyanide poisoning. Cook the berries before consuming them. The western variety, *S. racemosa*, with red berries may be more toxic than blue and black berries of the varieties *S. cerulean*, *S. canadensis*, and *S. nigra*. Avoid eating red elderberries; the fresh berry juice has caused illness. Ripe, cooked berries (pulp and skin) of most species of Sambucus are edible, but most uncooked berries and other parts of plants from this genus are potentially poisonous.

JEWELWEED, SPOTTED TOUCH-ME-NOTS

Basalminaceae (*Impatiens capensis* Meerb.)

Jewelweed

Identification: Fleshy annual that grows in dense colonies. Plant can reach 7′ in height. Stems are simple, light green, almost translucent, with swollen nodes. Leaves are deep green, thin and ovate, with 5–14 teeth. Flowers are ½″–¾″ in length; orange yellow with reddish-brown spots; spur shaped, irregular, with the spur curving back, lying parallel to the sac. Fruit is oblong capsule that bursts open when ripe and disperses seeds.

Habitat: Widespread east of the Rockies; incidental in the West. Found in lowlands, wetlands, fens, along edges of lakes, streams, and bogs.

Food: Eat the small flowers of summer in salads and stir-fries. The young shoots of spring form a ground cover in wet lowlands and along streams, wetlands, and lakes. Pick the shoots and add them to your mushroom soup and egg dishes, or stir-fry or sauté them with spring vegetables.

Traditional uses: As a traditional treatment for poison ivy, crush and rub the aerial parts of jewelweed over the inflamed area—the plant juices immediately reduce itching as well as inflammation. Native Americans used jewelweed for treating dyspepsia, measles, and hives. The Creek used an infusion of smashed spicebush berries and jewelweed as a bath for congestive heart failure. The crushed flowers placed over bruises, cuts, and burns.

Modern uses: The whole herb is infused as an appetite stimulant and diuretic. Naturopaths administer it to treat dyspepsia. Use of the herb as a therapy for relieving itch and inflammation caused by poison ivy proven—try it (see Meuninck, Clark, and Roman 2007).

Notes: I grow jewelweed in my garden for greens, edible flowers, and its anti-inflammatory qualities (treats poison ivy, poison sumac, and poison oak). Gather seeds in fall and spread them in a low-lying area of your garden, then get out of the way. It's aggressive and spreads. In the wild, it grows in dense colonies, often with stinging nettle, and is indicated to treat nettle rash.

Lobelia siphilitica

LOBELIA

Campanulaceae *(Lobelia siphilitica L.)*

Identification: Plant is 3'–4' high with oval leaves. Flower distinctive, birdlike, typically blue to blue lavender; throat of corolla is white striped. Plant has simple, alternate leaves and 2-lipped tubular flowers, each with 5 lobes. The upper 2 lobes may be erect, while the lower 3 lobes may be fanned out. Flowering is often abundant, and the flower color is striking and intense.

Habitat: There are numerous species from coast to coast, including subalpine varieties. Find *L. siphilitica* in moist areas, streamside, bogs, fens, and wetlands of all sorts. Alpine varieties are often found on dry slopes where melting snow fields have given the flowers the push to ignite in full color.

Food: Not used as food; toxic.

Traditional uses: Lobelia was used to induce vomiting and increase respiration, and as a narcotic and analgesic (to treat toothache). *L. siphilitica* used with *Podophyllum peltatum* (mayapple) to treat venereal diseases. Traditionally, various species of lobelia used for treating dysentery, cirrhosis, gastroenteritis, edema, eczema, and schistosomiasis. A poultice of root rubbed on sore neck muscles and back muscles. Both roots and leaves used as an external detoxifier and analgesic on bites and stings, boils, and sores. A cold infusion of plant is a strong emetic. Smoking lobelia considered a foul-tasting cure for cigarette smoking, but fatalities may occur if the practitioner is not skilled in the use of the herb.

Modern uses: Patents protect several alkaloids derived from various lobelia species, including lobeline, lobelanidine, lobelanine, and their various salts. These patented chemicals are potential drugs to treat psychostimulant abuse and eating disorders, and possibly cocaine abuse as well as abuse of amphetamines, caffeine, opiates, barbiturates, benzodiazepines, cannabinoids, hallucinogens, alcohol, and phencyclidine.

Note: I transplanted *L. siphilitica* to a shaded area of my garden—an attractive medicinal addition.

CAUTION: This is a very potent and potentially toxic herb. Do not experiment with it.

Lobelia cardinalis; L., the cardinal flower

MINT, PEPPERMINT

Lamiaceae *(Mentha arvensis; Mentha piperita* L.)

Identification: Members of the mint family have common characteristics including a square stem, leaves that are almost always aromatic when crushed, typically aggressive and invasive. Root is a spreading rhizome. Leaves are typically shiny, lance shaped, ovate to roundish, usually serrated. Flowers in dense whorls culminate in a terminal spike of blossoms with some variability; for example, *M. arvensis* has whorls of flowers rising up the stem in leaf axils. Flower colors vary by species: white, violet, or blue.

Habitat: Found nationwide around water, dunes of the Great Lakes, and around mountain passes, blow-downs (wind flattened trees), avalanche slides, and wet meadows.

Food: Peppermint leaf and flowers are used in teas, salads, and cold drinks; with sautéed vegetables;

Mentha arvensis

and as an integral part of the Indian subcontinent and Middle Eastern flavor principles. Romans such as Pliny the Elder used mint to flavor wines and sauces. Mint is excellent in Mexican bean soups or in chilled soups of all kinds.

Traditional uses: Aristotle considered peppermint an aphrodisiac, and Alexander the Great thought eating mint or drinking mint tea caused listless, unaggressive behavior. Peppermint leaves and flowers infused in water make a mood-elevating tea. The extracted oil (as well as the tea) is antiseptic, carminative, warming, and relieves muscle spasms. An infusion increases perspiration and stimulates bile secretion. Menthol and menthone, peppermint's inherent volatile oils, are antibacterial, antiseptic, antifungal, cooling, and anesthetic to the skin. In too high a concentration, the oils are a skin irritant and may burn—be careful.

Modern uses: Leaf and flower extraction are Commission E–approved for treating dyspepsia and gallbladder and liver problems. Peppermint oil is approved for colds, coughs, bronchitis, fevers, mouth and larynx inflammations, infection prevention, dyspepsia, and gallbladder and liver problems. Recent studies in Europe suggest it may be a treatment for irritable bowel syndrome. The tea and oil have an antispasmodic effect on the digestive system. Peppermint leaves and extractions are used to treat colic, cramps, and flatulence. It may help relieve diarrhea, spastic colon, and constipation (GR). Headache due to digestive weakness is relieved by taking peppermint, and trials using the diluted essential oil rubbed on temples to relieve headaches and tension look promising. Diluted mint oil is used in aromatherapy for treating headache and as an inhalant for respiratory infections—rubbed on the chest. Mint capsules are used to relieve irritable bowel syndrome and to relieve colon spasms during enema procedures (NIH). *Mentha arvensis* in mouse models protected the rodents from gamma radiation. It exhibited enhanced antibiotic activity against multiresistant *E. coli* and *Staphylococcus aureus* bacteria. It shows antifertility and abortive activity in mice (Meuninck 2007; Continho et al. 2009).

Notes: Peppermint, spearmint, mountain mint, and other mints have edible flowers and leaves. I use them in salads and desserts. Try mint blossoms on sliced pears. Mint is a carminative, and mint lozenges may quell discomfort from irritable bowel syndrome. Gardeners beware: Grow mints in a buried steel container to prevent their unabated spread.

PAPER BIRCH, WHITE BIRCH

Betulaceae (*Betula papyrifera* Marsh.)

Identification: Brown-barked sapling that matures into white-barked tree of medium height. Peeling, paper-like bark separates into layers clearly marked with horizontal stripes. Twigs are slightly rough, warty, odorless. Leaf buds blunt, hairless. Leaves heart shaped, 1"–4" long. Fruiting catkins are flowers. Paper birch is also known as white birch.

Habitat: Across the northern tier of the United States, throughout Canada, and in the southern half of Alaska. Found in loamy to sandy well-drained soil, in and around lowland and alpine areas.

Food: White birch and yellow birch (*B. alleghaniensis*) are tapped for their sap in late winter and early spring.

Traditional uses: White birch considered by Native Americans and herbalists as a tonic and blood purifier. Bark powder used to treat diaper rash and other skin rashes. The Cree used the bark powder to treat chapping and venereal disease. The Ojibwas used it for stomach cramps. The outer bark used as a poultice to cover wounds and as a cast for broken limbs. Wood shavings prepared in decoction stimulate lactation. A decoction of the ends of stems and new growth treated toothache and teething. The inner bark used in decoction for treating diarrhea. The decoction of new-growth tips of branches used as a tonic. Stomach cramps treated with decocted root bark mixed with maple syrup. Sap used to treat coughs.

Modern uses: Birch leaf extract is Commission E–approved for urinary tract infections, rheumatism, and bladder and kidney stones. Do not take if you have edema, heart disease, or kidney dysfunction. Betulic acid made from the bark extraction; betulin is being tested as an anticancer drug.

White birch

Notes: Shredded from the tree, the bark makes an excellent survival fire starter (right after cattail fluff and bone-dry grass). In winter, the tough bark peeled and stretched over a canoe frame made of white cedar and pine to make birch-bark canoes; balsam resin is used to seal seams. Rotten birch wood is useful for smoking foods.

SWEET FLAG, CALAMUS

Acoraceae *(Acorus calamus L.)*
Identification: Perennial about 2' tall that grows from a rhizome. Stem composed of long swordlike leaves arranged in 2 rows. Primitve looking green flowers on a club-like spadix. Entire plant has an intense, sweet aroma and grows in large colonies.

Acorus calamus

Habitat: Typically east of the Mississippi River in wetlands, along creeks, marshes, lakes, wet roadsides, and streams.

Food: Not edible.

Traditional uses: Sweet flag was considered the number-one herb both for medicine and ritual use among seven eastern Native American tribes. During the sun dance ceremony, when First Peoples may sing for 10 hours or more, they put a piece of calamus root between the cheek and gum to keep their throats moist. The root is a sialagogue; that is, it induces mouth glands to secrete juices. Sweet flag leaf garlands worn by Native Americans as fragrant necklaces to mask body odors. The root tea is an appetite stimulant. The aromatic, bitter root is a stomach tonic to relieve dyspepsia and gastritis. The root chewed for toothache. For centuries, the plant used as a nervine, sedative, and relaxant. The root traditionally chewed or prepared in decoction by pioneers to treat colds, coughs, fevers, children's colic and congestion. The dried and powdered rhizome inhaled to treat congestion and considered an antispasmodic, anticonvulsant, and possible central nervous system depressant.

Modern uses: The extract from the peeled and dried rhizome is carminative, tonic, antispasmodic, and stimulant (GR). It increases sweating. In vitro studies suggest that it is anticlotting and that it may aid in treating aggressive and impulsive behavior. The extract is also considered a sedative (GR). In traditional Chinese medicine, the root extract used internally to treat gastrointestinal complaints and externally to treat fungal infections. A few Asians consider it an aphrodisiac. Triploid strains in Europe and the United States are used to treat ulcers; the triploid strain produces about one-third the amount of beta asarone as the tetraploid strain from India. Kalmus root oil (*A. calamus* var. *americanus*) is still used as bitters to relieve stomach spasms and a distended stomach with a concurrent headache associated with poor digestion. According to Andrew Chevallier (1996), *A. calamus* var. *americanus* does not contain as much of the carcinogenic beta asarone. Animal studies suggest that the root extract may lower serum cholesterol. See http://www.ajbpr.com/issues/volume1/issue4/FINAL%208.pdf.

Notes: A few herbalists chew or suck the dried root to keep them awake on long drives. Put about a pound of the fresh, crushed, and chopped root in a pair of clean panty hose and submerge it in a hot bath or Jacuzzi—it's aromatic and relaxing. The dried and ground rhizome and root hairs are a spice and fragrance in food, but because of the beta asarone content, this use is discouraged in the United States. An exotic aromatic useful in flower arranging, the plant is an interesting addition to the garden. I located a particular striking stand along the north side of US 12 just east of White Pigeon, Michigan. According to locals, Potawatomi harvested the stand for hundreds of years.

CAUTION: Beta asarone is carcinogenic and a component of *A. calamus* that when taken in ample amounts over time induced cancer in laboratory animals. Therapeutic doses of the triploid strain must be professionally monitored. Avoid long-term use. Use only under the administration of skilled holistic health-care practitioner. Follow recommended dosages on the package.

TAMARACK, AMERICAN LARCH
Pinaceae *(Larix larcina* Du Boi, K. Koch.)*

Identification: Medium to large deciduous tree that at a distance looks like a pine (it is a primitive pine). Bark flakes off in scales. American larch has nondrooping branches (in contrast, the European larch has drooping branches). Needles are slender to 1" long, in clusters, single or several, emanating from short spurs on branches. Cones less than ¾" long.

Habitat: Northern wetlands, from southern Michigan north. The bald cypress is a similar species found in wet areas of the southern United States.

Food: Infuse new shoots into water to make tea, or panfry as food. Scrape the inner bark free, dry, and pound into flour—reconstitute with water to make flatbread.

Traditional uses: Native Americans used a decoction of tamarack-bark extraction in combination with balsam resin and other plants to treat acute infections such as colds, flu, fever, and coughs. Various tribes used the bark infusion of young shoots as a laxative. A bark-and-wood poultice applied over wounds to draw out infection. The inner bark infusion is warming. The resinous balsam used as a stimulating inhalant. Native Americans pounded and crushed the leaf and bark, and applied the mass as a poultice to reduce headache. This ritual sweat-lodge plant is useful for relieving tension, backache, and headache; its needles, twigs, and bark dampened and applied

Larix larcina

to hot stones to produce steam. Western larch, *L. occidentalis*, found in the Rockies to the West Coast, used in similar ways, including a decoction of the new growth as a wash for cancer. The resinous pitch of the western species mixed with animal fat and used on wounds, cuts, and burns.

Modern uses: *L. decidua*, tamarack's European cousin, is Commission E–approved to treat coughs, colds, bronchitis, and fever, and to promote resistance to acute infections. The outer-bark extraction and balsam (resin) are used to make ointments, gels, and other emulsions for external application.

Notes: This rot-resistant relative of cypress makes long-lived railroad ties. The tree's tough, fibrous, and rot-resistant roots provide material for sewing and for weaving baskets. Bark used to sew birch bark together to make canoes. Feed the shredded inner bark to horses.

WATERCRESS
Brassicaceae *(Nasturtium officinale* L.*)*
Identification: Water-loving plant that grows in mud-rooted floating mats. Grooved stem is tough and fibrous when mature. Leaves are alternate, ovate, with paired and lobed leaflets. Each leaflet is broader toward the base and about ¾" wide, but variable in width, with terminal lobe. White flowers are ¼" wide, with

Watercress

4 petals; blooms in May and sporadically throughout summer.

Habitat: Found nationwide in temperate areas in or near seeps and springs, along the margins of slow-moving, muck-bottomed streams and creeks.

Food: Watercress is from the mustard family, and its taste is spicy and pungent. Harvest watercress from a *clean* water source and then cook. Trust only your backyard if you plan to eat this food raw. Pull watercress out by its roots and replant it in your garden. Keep it wet, and it will reward you with peppery leaves. One of the main ingredients in V8 vegetable juice, watercress is great in Italian dishes: Try it half and half with spinach in lasagna. Secret sources provide my family edible leaves year-round.

Traditional uses: A pharmaceutical record all the way back to Hippocrates describes watercress as a heart tonic, stimulating expectorant, and digestive. It is good for coughs, colds, and bronchitis and relieves gas. As a diuretic, it releases fluid retention and cleanses the kidneys and bladder. Mexicans revere this plant as a spring tonic. Dampen the aerial parts and grill over charcoal.

Modern uses: Watercress is a good source of vitamins, minerals, and isothiocyanate (GR); isothiocyanate may provide protection from cancer and is Commission E–approved to treat coughs and bronchitis.

Notes: Relocate watercress found growing in questionable water sources to your garden. Keep it well watered and it will cleanse itself. A spring near my home has more than 3 acres of watercress—a multimillion-dollar crop living out its life in a hallowed sanctuary. One of the first plants of spring, seek it for its nutritional and health-protecting benefits.

WILLOWS: WHITE WILLOW, BLACK WILLOW, SWAMP WILLOW

Salicaceae *(Salix* spp.; *S. alba* L.; *S. nigra* Marsh.*)*

Salix alba

Identification: Tree or shrub with lance-like, fine-toothed leaves; yellow male flowers and green female flowers in the form of densely blossomed catkins. *S. alba*, sometimes called weeping willow, has drooping branches. *S. nigra* (black willow) is erect and large with shedding branches. Both prefer wet ground and are considered dirty trees, as they constantly shed branches, flowers, and leaves.

Habitat: Found nationwide in marshy areas, thickets, lakeshores, and along streams and rivers.

Food: A tea from the twig bark contains salicin (an aspirin-like compound). Use it with extreme care as an analgesic and anti-inflammatory.

Traditional uses: Native Americans used the bark of twigs and new growth in decoction to treat tendonitis, arthritis, headaches, and bursitis. An infusion of the stem and leaves releases salicin, the chemical model for synthetic aspirin. Aspirin may help prevent acute infections, cancer, strokes, and heart attacks. It may help boost immunity, but it does have numerous side effects and may aggravate ulcers and cause intestinal bleeding.

Modern uses: The extraction, although infrequently used from the tree, is Commission E–approved for treating pain and rheumatism.

Notes: Do not garden under or near a willow. Willow rootlets travel near the surface and suck water and nutrients from the soil, distressing garden plants grown around them. When a willow dies, be aware that the widespread root system has drained the soil of nutrients. Rebuild the soil before you replant the area.

CAUTION: Don't use if allergic to salicylates. Keep in mind that the infusion or decoction of willow contains much more than salicin. Recent evidence shows that willow can concentrate cadmium, a toxic metal; all species of willow concentrate this metal when available in the soil. Use aspirin, not willow, for its therapeutic effects.

Chapter Four: Medicinal Plants of Yards, Prairies, Roadsides, and Meadows

Many of the most useful herbs known to man grow right outside the door. They are robust, aggressive, prolific plants that provide energy and health-protecting chemistry.

Balm Melissa (Melissa), 48

Bee Balm (Monarda), 49

Burdock (Arctium), 50

Chicory (Cichorium), 51

Catnip (Nepeta), 52

Curly Dock (Rumex), 53

Dandelion (Taraxacum), 54

Echinacea (Echinacea), 55

Evening Primrose (Oenothera), 56

Flax (Linum), 57

Foxglove (Digitalis), 58

Goldenrod (Solidago), 59

Heal-All (Prunella), 60

Jimsonweed (Datura), 61

Marijuana (Cannabis), 62

Motherwort (Leonurus), 63

Mullein (Verbascum), 64

Passionflower (Passiflora), 65

Plantain (Plantago), 66

Red Clover (Trifolium), 67

Saint-John's-Wort (Hypericum), 68

Stinging Nettle (Urtica), 69

Yarrow (Achillea), 70

BALM MELISSA, LEMON BALM

Melissa officinalis

Lamiaceae *(Melissa officinalis L.)*
Identification: A 2'–3' many-branched perennial that is aromatic, lemony. Stems are erect, square, hairy to hairless. Leaves have petioles and are oval to rhomboid shaped and plentiful. Leaves lemon scented (touch and sniff). Plant produces numerous small, white, 2-lipped flowers on the end of an upcurved corolla tube. Flowers localized in one-sided false whorls in upper axils of leaves. Seeds are nut brown. Flowers bloom in summer.

Habitat: A garden plant that escaped to roadsides and vacant lots and fields. Ask your herb-growing friends to show you this plant, which is also available from garden stores. Worth having!

Food: Use flowers and leaf buds in salads, desserts, and toppings and cooked with vegetables. Mature, aromatic balm leaves can be used in baths. Infused as a tea or infused in cream to make balm ice cream (remove leaves before freezing). A cold infusion with other mints is excellent: Stuff a jar with lemon balm leaves, other mint leaves, thyme leaves, and 2 slices of lemon; refrigerate overnight. The addition of thyme leaves make this a robust tea for mountaineers, protecting them from mountain sickness.

Traditional uses: In traditional Chinese medicine lemon balm cooling is in the second degree (opens pores and thins fluids), like chamomile, mint, valerian, passion flower. This relaxing nervine calms the central nervous system. First leaves of spring and flowers of summer dried and packaged as tea. In China, 1–4 g of dried aerial parts taken in decoction 3 times per day are used to treat stress. Lemon balm is a peripheral vasodilator and cooling to fevers; historically used to reduce blood pressure (unproven).

Modern uses: Phytochemicals in lemon balm relax autonomic muscles in the digestive tract and uterus. It is a sleep aid, reducing mental stress (CM). As a calming digestive, the tea relieves headaches and toothaches and is Commission E–approved for insomnia and nervous agitation. German studies suggest that citral and citronellal in lemon balm relax the central nervous system. Polyphenolic compounds are antiviral, used specifically on *herpes simplex* (cold sores). High doses of pure lemon balm extracts are effective in reducing stress in human subjects, producing increased ratings of calmness and alertness. It increases in the speed of mathematical processing, with no reduction in accuracy after a 300 mg dose of extract. In one study, it reduced oxidative stress in radiologists exposed to persistent low-dose radiation. After 30 days of taking the tea daily, researchers found that it resulted in a significant improvement as an antioxidant, raising plasma levels of catalase, superoxide dismutase, and glutathione peroxidase—while reducing plasma DNA damage and lipid peroxidation. Lemon balm preparations improve mood and mental performance. These effects involve muscarinic and nicotinic acetylcholine receptors. Positive results have been achieved in a small clinical trial involving Alzheimer's. (For research citations see www.en.wikipedia.org/wiki/Melissa_officinalis.)

Notes: Crushed leaves, when rubbed on the skin, repel mosquitoes. Lemon balm is an aggressive garden herb, at first rewarding and then a nuisance. I cannot drink enough tea to keep up with it, but I cannot live without it either.

CAUTION: Lemon balm inhibits the absorption of the thyroid medication thyroxine. Naturopaths use it to treat overactive thyroid. Do not use if pregnant or lactating, as it is a uterine stimulant.

BEE BALM, WILD BERGAMONT, HORSEMINT
Lamiaceae (*Monarda fistulosa* L.; *Monarda didyma* L.)

Monarda didyma

Identification: A 3′, erect perennial of the mint family. Straight stem is grooved and hard; oval to lance-shaped leaves in pairs, rough on both sides. Both species have flowers in 1–3 false whorls; flowers are horn shaped—pluck one and notice its resemblance to a stork's head and neck. *M. didyma* has red flowers, and *M. fistulosa* has blue flowers. Red *M. didyma* florets taste pineapple-like, weakly oregano flavored, whereas *M. fistulosa* has a strong oregano flavor.

Habitat: *M. didyma* found in wet areas from Georgia through Michigan and into Canada. *M. fistulosa* grows across the nation, often along trails in the Rockies and Cascades and roadsides in Michigan, Indiana, and throughout the East, usually in well-drained areas, but it will tolerate both wet and dryness.

Monarda fistulosa

Food: *M. fistulosa* is the stronger tasting, more of a condiment. Eat young leaves raw, cook leaves with other dishes for flavoring, add flowers to salads or tea. Either is excellent as a garnish over sauces (and a flavoring agent in sauce), especially Italian. Use both species to season meats for drying and/or smoking. Add *M. fistulosa* flowers to black tea to get an Earl Grey–like flavor.

Traditional uses: Navahos considered *M. fistulosa* lightning medicine and gunshot medicine—a powerful warrior plant. Infuse *M. didyma* in hot water to make

Oswego tea. *M. fistulosa* has a stronger flavor. Both plants used by Native Americans as a carminative, abortifacient, cold remedy, sedative, analgesic, hemostat, emetic, pulmonary aid, diaphoretic, to induce sweating, and to treat coughs and the flu. Pioneers used it to treat bronchial complaints, sinusitis, digestive problems, flatulence, and as an antirheumatic and expectorant. At one time *M. didyma* was used as an alternative to quinine.

Modern uses: *M. didyma* is used more widely. Its chemical constituents may provide protection from diseases of aging. Aerial parts in infusion have chemicals that may prevent acetylcholine (neural transmitter) breakdown. Modern holistic practitioners use the plant to treat menstrual cramps and other symptoms of premenstrual syndrome and as a digestive and antiflatulent. The tea from both herbs is stimulating—the garden's mental pick-me-up. *M. fistulosa* leaves and florets may be used to relieve pain of toothache and are somewhat antiseptic (GR). Bee balm infused into oil and used in aromatherapy is calming.

Notes: I eat up to 20 florets per day. Teas should contain several score of flowers for full flavor. I prefer *M. didyma* over *M. fistulosa* for salads and as a garnish. *M. fistulosa* is best in sauces and as a stimulating tea.

CAUTION: Not to be used during pregnancy or when lactating. If you have flower allergies, be careful when using bee balm flowers in salads and teas, although there have been no documented side effects.

Burdock

BURDOCK, GOBO BURDOCK

Asteraceae *(Arctium lappa L.)*
Identification: Biennial. Mature plant is many branched and spreading; to 7'–8' in height, often much smaller. First year's growth sprouts broad elephant ear–like leaves (heart shaped) directly from a deep taproot. Leaves are rough, lighter on the underside. Second-year leaves are slightly smaller. Crimson flowers have inward-curving bracts that eventually form the mature seed capsule, which is a burr. This is the plant that deposits burrs on your dog and your trousers.

Habitat: Northern Hemisphere, temperate zone. Gardens, roadsides, and disturbed ground—just about every place you walk your dog from East Coast to West Coast.

Food: Harvest roots in autumn or the spring of the first year's growth. Roots may be 20" long. Peel the root, and then slice diagonally (julienne) and stir-fry, steam, or sauté. Thinly slice root into frittatas and on homemade pizzas. Peel stem of first year's leaves, cook, and eat. Cut second-year flower spikes, peel, and then sauté or steam until tender.

Traditional uses: Polysaccharides in burdock roots treat immune-system deficiency. Use seed extract on skin conditions. Leaf infusion used to treat chronic skin problems; root oil used the same way. Prepare the oil by soaking the chopped root in olive oil in the refrigerator for 1 month. Eating the lightly cooked root helps regulate blood sugar and is considered antidiabetic. Root polysaccharides purportedly lower blood sugar by slowing the absorption of glucose from the intestines. Drinking the root tea and eating the root said to help treat acne. The root as food is a warming tonic and detoxifier said to strengthen the stomach, liver, and lymphatic system.

Modern uses: According to Japanese studies, the root is anticancer (antimutagenic) in animal studies. Chinese practitioners use leafy second-year branches in infusion to treat rheumatism, arthritis, and measles. This medicinal tea sweetened with raw cane sugar. Tincture of seeds has been used for treating psoriasis (CM), but personally, it did not help me. The essential oil from the seed reported to encourage hair growth and improve skin condition (CM) (not proven). One clinical study found that topical application of a formulation containing burdock extract visibly reduced wrinkles (Knott et al. 2008). A mixture of burdock and astragalus root reduced urinary protein and albumin, and improved lipid metabolism and postprandial blood glucose in patients with diabetic nephropathy (Wang and Chen 2004). Other clinical trials with humans are lacking in the literature.

Notes: To make a carbohydrate-rich broth, wash the roots, then pound or macerate them in warm water to release the polysaccharides, inulin, and mucilage. I eat copious amounts of the stir-fried root, but raw-root polysaccharides are difficult to digest. The root, called *gobo,* is purchased in Asian markets; it's free from your backyard if you plant it there. Simply pull burrs off a dog or your trousers after a walk, crush the burrs to release the seeds, and spread the seeds on scuffed soil in November. Plant thickly, and then thin and spread seedlings in May. By the way, burdock's seed-dispersal mechanism (curved spines) led to the invention of Velcro.

CAUTION: Avoid if pregnant or lactating. Seek holistic health-care consultation before using the herb to treat serious illness.

CHICORY

Asteraceae *(Cichorium intybus* L.)*

Identification: Biennial or perennial to 4' in height; stem erect, with few branches. Lance-shaped leaves in a basal whorl as well as additional smaller upper leaves. Blue flowers (rarely white or pink) with square tipped rays and a dandelion-like taproot.

Habitat: Nationwide on roadsides, fields, meadows, and waste ground.

Chicorum intybus

Food: Chicory root is dried, roasted, ground, and mixed with coffee beans to yield Cajun coffee. The flower petals are slightly bitter and add a nice flavor construct when stirred into cottage cheese (let the blossoms infuse into the cheese overnight in the refrigerator) and are healthful additions to salads, jump-starting the digestion process.

Traditional uses: The root, dried or fresh, in a water decoction was used as diuretic, dietetic, and laxative. Root tea stimulates digestion, improving both peristalsis and

Edible chicory flower

absorption. Root decoction was used externally to treat fever blisters. Cherokees used root infusion as a tonic for the nerves.

Modern uses: Homeopathic practitioners use a diluted dose to treat gallbladder and liver complaints. Commission E–approved for stimulating appetite and dyspepsia. Root decoction may reduce blood sugar (GR). Root constituents are antibacterial in vitro. Chicory's anti-inflammatory activity is under investigation. Root drug may slow heart rate and reduce heart thrust. Animal studies showed a cholesterol-lowering effect. In India, the root decoction used to treat headaches, vomiting, and diarrhea. In animal studies, chicory extract showed anti-inflammatory activity (Balbaa et al. 1973). Chicory has shown antihepatoxic activity in animal studies (Hassan and Yousef 2010).

Notes: This is a must-have, attractive garden flower with edible leaves, edible flowers, and a system-stimulating root. The leaf extraction is less bitter than the root decoction and evokes a milder response.

Nepeta cataria

CATNIP

Lamiaceae *(Nepeta cataria* L.)
Identification: Perennial that grows to 3½′ in height with erect and many-branched stems. Leaves are grayish green, giving plant a whitish-gray appearance, 1′–3″ long, ovate, serrated, with gray underside. Leaf petiole is 1½″ long. Flower spike has large cluster of individual flowers attached with short pedicels.

Habitat: Found nationwide in gardens, roadsides, and waste ground; tolerates well-drained, dry areas.

Food: Leaves and flowers used fresh or dried, in tea as a relaxing drink or for treatment.

Traditional uses: Aerial parts of the plant in infusion are a bitter, astringent, and cooling antispasmodic (relaxant). Catnip leaf and flower teas provide a mild sedative effect. It is antiflatulent and may settle a colicky baby; check with your holistic health-care professional before using it in this manner. It can be used to soothe the digestive tract, and it may provide relief from menstrual cramps by mildly stimulating menstruation. The herbal tea promotes sweating, thereby lowering fever in acute infections. Like many herbal teas, it is a mild diuretic.

Modern uses: Tea used to stimulate the gallbladder (GR). Naturopaths use catnip to treat colic and stomachache in children (CM). According to Andrew Chevallier (1996), catnip may be tinctured and used as a rub for rheumatic and arthritic joints. Naturopaths combine catnip leaves with elderberry flowers for treating acute infections. As a sleep aid, another combination is catnip, valerian root, and hops; this combination is used to reduce stress and as a relaxant. There are few studies verifying the effects of smoking catnip. Anecdotal evidence suggests it is a relaxing pain-moderating smoke (Osterhoudt et al. 1997).

Notes: I prefer catnip tea prepared from the fresh herb in a cold infusion, as its physiologically active constituents are volatile and reduced by drying. Typical dosage is 3 cups per day. Catnip is a cat's drug of choice. Start catnip indoors and transplant it when it is at least 1' tall—then maybe it will survive the onslaught of drug-seeking felines! Actinidine, an iridoid glycoside in catnip, stimulates a cat's brain.

CAUTION: Do not use during pregnancy or while lactating.

CURLY DOCK, YELLOW DOCK, GREATER WATER DOCK

Polygonaceae (Rumex crispus L.*; Rumex orbiculatus* A. Gray)

Curled dock, **Rumex crispus**

Identification: Perennials from a stout, unbranched stem with long, wavy (curved margins) lance-shaped leaves. Basal leaves larger, higher leaves shorter and more narrow. Leaves long stalked, alternate, and have a sour to bitter taste. Flower spikes to 3', with large clusters of green(then brown) flowers on branched clusters, several clusters branching from central stalk. Greater water dock is taller (to 10') and found in wetlands. *R. crispus* blooms June to September and greater water dock blooms in July. Both have large, deep, yellowish roots.

Habitat: Found nationwide in fringes of yards, stream sides, vacant lots, and roadsides.

Food: Eat young leaves steamed, sautéed, or stir-fried. Be judicious, as leaves may be bitter. Try steaming the herbs, then frying them in olive oil. Eat the inner pulp of the flowering stem after cooking—squeeze pulp from the skin to reduce bitterness. Seeds are plentiful and may be gathered and made into a mush.

Traditional uses: Pioneers considered the plant to be an excellent blood purifier, a spring tonic for whatever ails you. Native Americans mashed the root and applied it to the skin to treat arthritis. Cherokees used the root juice to treat diarrhea. One unusual use was rubbing the outside of the throat with a crushed leaf to treat sore throat. Cooked seeds eaten to stem diarrhea. Dried and powdered root used to stop bleeding (styptic).

Greater water dock, **Rumex orbiculatus**

Modern uses: Holistic practitioners combine dock with dandelion root to treat skin problems. *PDR for Herbal Medicines*, 4th edition (2007), notes yellow dock is a mild tonic and laxative. Naturopaths simmer the sliced root and administer the broth to pregnant women as a source of iron without causing constipation often produced by taking elemental iron supplements. The bitter taste of the herb (root and leaves) stimulates digestion: It increases hydrochloric acid secretion, increases peristalsis, and improves secretion of other digestive enzymes, improving digestion and assimilation. Whole plant in decoction said to cleanse toxins from body and may have a laxative effect because of inherent constipation-relieving tannins and anthraquinones (GR). As food, reported to help improve chronic skin problems. Bitter taste stimulates liver activity (blood purifier) and may help cleanse the liver, thereby relieving related skin manifestations (GR).

Notes: Yellow dock or curly dock savages the garden. I dig them up and throw the lot on my mulch pile, where they take hold and grow some more. The plant scrubs minerals from the soil, providing soil-enriching mulch. Simmer the root (fresh or dried) and steal the minerals for yourself. Spaniards eat the plant for its vitamin C content and use it as a mild laxative and diuretic.

CAUTION: Restrict the amount of dock leaves you eat because of the high tannin and oxalic acid content. These chemicals may be harmful to the kidneys when eaten in excess; once a week is optimal.

DANDELION

Asteraceae *(Taraxacum officinale* **G. H. Weber ex Wiggers***)*

Identification: Perennial herb with a basal whorl of toothed leaves and a deep bitter-tasting taproot. It displays a yellow composite flower with numerous rays born on a 6"–10" flower stem (petiole). The torn leaf or flower petiole exudes white-colored latex.

Habitat: Temperate regions worldwide; common yard bounty.

Food: A vitamin- and mineral-rich salad green. Tear small pieces from tough veins and add to a mix of thyme, fennel, nasturtiums, and salad greens. Thyme and fennel balance the dandelion's bitterness. Make a mineral-rich tea from dandelion roots and leaves. Gently simmer chopped fresh roots for a stomach bitters; the bitter brew will stimulate the flow of gastric acid and bile, improving digestion and assimilation. Cook fresh leaves gathered early in the season with olive oil, bacon, and lemon juice. As the season progresses, dandelion leaves become more bitter: Pour copious amount of water on the late-summer plants so that the morning harvest will be sweeter. Even when bitter, the leaves are a healthy addition to stir-fries. Try dandelion with tofu; cook them in oyster oil with cayenne, garlic, and beef strips.

Taraxacum officinale

Traditional uses: The root decoction is a liver-cleansing tonic that aids digestion and helps cleanse the blood. It is also diuretic and traditionally used to treat premenstrual syndrome (PMS). It has a mild laxative effect and may relieve inflammation and congestion of the gallbladder and liver. Native Americans applied a poultice of steamed leaves to treat stomachaches. Greens considered a tonic blood purifier. The root decoction was drunk to increase lactation and used as mild laxative and for dyspepsia.

Modern uses: Commission E–approved for treating dyspeptic complaints, urinary infections, liver and gallbladder complaints, and appetite loss. Root extract may lower cholesterol and blood pressure (hypotensive). Dandelion is one of the most potent diuretics (GR). Its performance in animal studies is equal to the prescription drug furosemide. Dandelions are a stimulating tonic and mild laxative with the capacity to regulate blood glucose (WHO). The bitter taste of dandelion is an appetite stimulant and stimulates the entire digestive system (cholagogue), improves appetite, and may be helpful treating anorexia (NIH). It raises hydrochloric acid secretion in the stomach, improving calcium breakdown and absorption, and it also spurs bile production (CM).

Notes: Dandelion and other bitter high-fiber greens can theoretically lower cholesterol in three ways: (1) Eating the leaves stimulates the secretion of bile, requiring more production of bile from cholesterol in the liver; (2) fiber in the plants locks up bile in the digestive tract, arresting cholesterol breakdown and emulsification, thus preventing cholesterol absorption; and (3) fiber removes bile from body, causing the liver to break down more cholesterol to make more bile. These factors help prevent atherosclerosis, reduce stroke, and lower blood pressure. We eat dandelion greens and make root tea year-round. Bring plants indoors for the winter. Eight plants grown under lights or in a window provide ample edible leaves for 2 people. Chop late-season bitter leaves and add to salads. Flower petals may be sprinkled over salads, rice dishes, and vegetable dishes.

ECHINACEA, PURPLE CONEFLOWER

Asteraceae (*Echinacea purpurea* [L.] Moench; *E. angustifolia* DC.)

Identification: Erect perennial to 2½' in height. Leaves 3"–4" long, opposite or alternate, with smooth (entire), toothed, or serrate margins and rough surface. Fibrous taproot when sliced shows yellowish center flecked with black, covered in thin bark-like skin. Purple blossoms are large, solitary, with spreading rays. Bracts are rigid, with thorn-like tips.

Echinacea in the Black Hills

Habitat: Eastern and central United States in meadows and prairies, fringes of fields and parks. Grown in gardens nationwide.
Food: Not used as food.
Traditional uses: Native Americans used root and flowers as a snakebite treatment. Boiled root water used to treat sore throats. Plant mashed and applied to wounds as a therapy for infections. Root infusion once considered a treatment for gonorrhea. Root masticated and held over sore tooth to treat infection.

Modern uses: Commercial preparations of roots, leaves, and flowers are used to treat colds, flu, coughs, bronchitis, fever, urinary infections, inflammations of the mouth and pharynx, weakened immune function, and wounds and burns (GR). Commission E–approved for wounds and burns, colds, coughs, bronchitis, urinary tract infections, mouth and throat inflammations, and infection prophylaxis. Echinacea therapy appears useful if started immediately at the onset of upper respiratory infections, taken 3 times a day and continued until the person is well. Echinacea enhances immunity in several ways. Polysaccharide-initiated response follows a bell curve: steep initial activity, improving immune response up to 32 percent. Then response peaks and after 4–6 days tapers off. Therefore, echinacea is useful for acute instead of chronic conditions. Note that a study published in 2005 challenged echinacea's immune-modulating effect (Schwarz et al. 2005). Echinacea extract administered internally to treat skin diseases, and fungal infections including both Candida and Listeria) as well as slow-healing wounds, boils, gangrene, upper respiratory tract infections, and sinusitis. Used externally for acne and psoriasis (not proven by this sufferer). Root oil has inhibited leukemia cells in vitro and vivo studies. Numerous studies show echinacea extract shortens the duration and severity of colds (Block and Mead 2003).

Notes: I have prepared an alcohol tincture of *E. purpurea* flowers as a gargle for mouth and tongue ulcers. I use it to prevent colds and the flu. A few years ago, I had a staphylococcal infection (cellulitis), an imbedded cyst in my buttock. My physician wanted to cut it out before it burst and infected other parts of my body. Instead I tried the echinacea floral extraction. The large cyst-like infection disappeared in 3 days and has not returned. I continued the therapy for a total of 6 days.

CAUTION: A study of 412 pregnant Canadian women (206 who took echinacea during pregnancy) showed that spontaneous abortions (13) were twice as frequent in the echinacea group. Consult your physician before using echinacea while pregnant (see http://www.ncbi.nlm.nih.gov/pubmed/11074744).

EVENING PRIMROSE

Onagraceae *(Oenothera biennis* L.)
Identification: Erect biennial that grows to 3' with turnip-like root. Leaves with short, hanging petioles, oblong lance shaped, pointed, and finely toothed. Solitary

yellow flowers in the leaf axils, 1"–1½" long, lower flowers open below buds. Flowers are fragrant and open in evening. Seed receptacle is long, linear, quadrangular shaped like an elongated vase from which gray to black seeds can be poured upon maturity.

Habitat: Widely spread throughout North America in gardens, roadsides, and meadows.

Food: The root is edible (as a biennial plant, the first-year root is better). New leaves of first or second year edible in salads and stir-fries.

Oenothera biennis

Seeds pour from seed capsule, which looks like small, dried okra pod. Immature seed capsules are cooked like okra; fair tasting.

Traditional uses: Cherokee used plant as food to lose weight and as a poultice for piles. Chewed roots provided strength. Potawatomi used seeds for treating various ailments. Poultice of the whole plant was placed over bruises.

Modern uses: The essential fatty acids and amino acids in the seeds are reportedly good for treating depression and psoriasis. I have psoriasis and have found this oil and borage oil expensive and ineffective ways to treat this autoimmune disease. I have more success at less cost using fish oil capsules, taking EPA and DHA, 1000 mg tablets, up to 12 per day, tapering down after 2 weeks to 6 per day and eventually 3 per day. This is not a cure but coupled with sun therapy and seawater bathing greatly clears my skin. Be certain to keep the skin moist with moisturizers. Other unsupported uses include treating cancer, arthritis, breast pain, preeclampsia. In one study, it reduced platelet aggregation in a human male population. Another study showed positive effects in treating diabetic neuropathy, and it may be helpful in relieving atopic eczema (NIH) (*PDR for Herbal Medicines* 2007).

Notes: A few sources recommend evening primrose oil for treating PMS.

FLAX, LINSEED

Linaceae (*Linum usitatissimum* L.)

Identification: Delicate-looking annual to 3' in height, typically shorter on waste ground. Gray-green leaves are lance shaped, smooth edged. Produces sky-blue flowers born in leaf axils on upper part of slender stem. Flowers have 5 sepals and 5 ovate petals with 5 stamens and 1 ovary; seeds are flat, brown, glossy.

Habitat: Temperate-zone plant found nationwide at roadsides,

Flax flower

barns, and waste ground near where the plant has escaped cultivation. Buy flaxseeds at a health-food store and spread them in your garden.

Food: Mix flaxseeds in salads, waffles, or pancakes; blend them into juice drinks; or eat them whole out of hand. ***Tip:*** Grind seeds before adding them to juice, cereal, and other foods to release the oils. They are healthful in corn bread, bread, and all baking, in fact, and are especially beneficial when used uncooked or very lightly cooked. See the DVD *Diet for Natural Health* (Meuninck et al. 2007) for numerous recipes using flax and other essential dietary fats. Flax flowers are edible. Add flaxseeds and cattail male reproductive parts to pizza dough mix (Meuninck 2013, 51).

Traditional uses: The Greeks and Romans considered flax a panacea. Native Americans used flax as food and medicine to treat inflammatory diseases and infections: colds, coughs, fevers, and painful urination. These early uses suggested the now-known anti-inflammatory effect of flax.

Modern uses: Flaxseed is one of highest plant sources of omega-3 fatty acids (perilla seeds at your Asian grocery contain slightly more omega-3). This essential fatty acid is a memory- and cognitive-mind enhancer. Omega-3s protect us from degenerative diseases and may prevent more autoimmune and inflammatory diseases. The husk of the seed has lignins, mucilage, and phenolics, providing extra protection from heart disease, cancer, and diabetes (GR) (CM). Flax is Commission E–approved for treating inflammations of the skin and constipation. Clinical trials have shown the efficacy of the supplement (oil) to lower cholesterol and raise plasma levels of insulin; as an antiplatelet aggregating agent it may decrease the potential for thrombosis (CM).

Notes: A physician friend claims not all people can convert the omega fats from flaxseeds into omega-3 fatty acids as efficiently as others. Eat cold-water fish—salmon, herring, sardines, and mackerel—or take fish-oil supplements as the preferred sources of these vital-essential fats. Take advice with a grain of salt, as the same physician sells a line of fish-oil supplements.

Digitalis purpurea

FOXGLOVE, PURPLE FOXGLOVE

Plantaginaceae *(Digitalis purpurea* L.)

Identification: Biennial, 3′–5′ in height with lance-shaped leaves, fuzzy (hairy) in basal rosette. Without the flower stalk, the basal rosette of leaves looks somewhat like mullein leaves or comfrey leaves, rarely dock leaves, but beware—the leaves of *Digitalis* are toxic. Flowers are thimble shaped, white to purple, aggregated on a spike, a long hanging raceme with white-edged spots on the inside. They look like gloves, hence the common name. Flowers bloom in the summer of second year.

Habitat: A common mountain wildflower along roadsides in Northwest and eastern mountain states. This is a favorite ornamental in gardens from coast to coast.

Food: Not edible; toxic.

Traditional uses: The powdered leaf contains potent cardiac glycosides perhaps first used by Celtic people in Europe. Overdose causes nausea, vomiting, slowed pulse, fainting, and possibly death (Meuninck 2014). Plant used externally on wounds and ulcers. Used in the British Isles to treat tumors, ulcers, headaches, and abscesses.

Modern uses: Homeopathic doses for cardiac insufficiency and migraine are available from licensed practitioners (*PDR for Herbal Medicines* 2007, 256). The plant-derived drug is obsolete; better synthetic, pure substances are used. The plant contains cardiac glycosides, used to model the now-synthesized drugs that increase heart thrust and lower venous pressure. It lowers the oxygen requirements of the heart and reduces frequency of heartbeat. Digitoxin has shown antitumor activity, reducing size of tumors in human patients (Stenkvist et al. 1980).

Notes: Transplants well to the garden and makes a striking plant. It tolerates some shade but prefers sun and well-drained soil.

CAUTION: Do not self-medicate with this attractive but dangerous plant.

GOLDENROD

**Asteraceae *(Solidago canadensis* L.)*

Identification: Perennial with numerous species that grows to 3'. *S. canadensis* is the most common eastern species, with a smooth stem at the base and hairy stem just below flower branches. Sharp-toothed leaves are plentiful, lance shaped, with 3 veins. Golden flowers line up atop the stem in a broad, branched spire or triangular-shaped cluster (panicle). Plant found most often in colonies, growing and spreading from rhizomes, flowering July through September.

Habitat: Nationwide in fields, meadows, roadsides, railroad rights-of-way, vacant lots, and edges of fields.

Food: Seeds, shoots, and leaves are edible. Flowers in small amounts made into a mild tea or used as a garnish on salads and other cold or hot dishes.

Solidago species

Traditional uses: Goldenrod is not the weed that causes autumn allergies—that's ragweed—but informants say that goldenrod tea made of fresh or dried flowers may protect a person from allergens (hypoallergenic). Dried leaves and flowers applied to wounds to stop bleeding (styptic). Traditional herbalists and pioneers used the tea to ward off acute infections like colds, flu, and bronchitis, as it induces the production of mucus.

Modern uses: In Europe, Commission E–approved for kidney and bladder stones as well as urinary tract infections. Plants gathered when in flower and then dried and used in Europe as a relaxant (spasmolytic) and anti-inflammatory. The drug is 6–12 g dried aerial parts in infusion. People with kidney and bladder problems should only use the herb under medical supervision. Whole-plant tea is a kidney tonic (diuretic) and may relieve nephritis (NIH) (GR).

Notes: According to the *PDR for Herbal Medicines,*4th edition (page 301)(2005), the herb "has a weak potential for sensitization (can cause allergies)." Plant drug rarely causes allergic reaction. Also, the whole plant may be infused and used as a yellow dye.

Prunella vulgaris

HEAL-ALL, SELF-HEAL
Lamiaceae *(Prunella vulgaris L.)*
Identification: A perennial typically 6"–10" tall. Square stem erect when young; may collapse and creep. Leaves ovate to lance shaped, margins vary from dentate (toothed) to entire (no teeth), and opposite. Blue to violet bract of flowers clustered in a whorl at end of square stem. Tubular 2-lipped flowers grow from a club-like cluster collared by a pair of stalkless leaves; top lip is a blue hood and bottom is often white.

Habitat: Nationwide in waste ground, lawns, edges of fields, and margins of woods.
Food: According to Moerman (1998, 439), the Cherokees cooked and ate the small leaves. The Thompson First People (Native Americans) made a cold infusion of the aerial parts and drank this as a common beverage. Self-heal has edible young leaves and stems—eat leaves raw in salads, or boil the whole plant and eat as a potherb. The aerial parts of the plant are dried, powdered, and then brewed in a cold infusion to make a tasty beverage.
Traditional uses: Documented use by the Chinese for more than 2,200 years for liver complaints and improving the function of the liver. The whole plant used in infusion to stimulate the liver and gallbladder and to promote healing. Considered an alternative, it may change the course of a chronic disease. Topically the whole plant poultice placed over wounds to promote healing. A mouthwash made from an infusion of the whole plant used to treat sore throats, thrush, and gum infections. Internally, tea treats diarrhea and internal bleeding (anecdotal).
Modern uses: Heal-all used internally by holistic practitioners to treat excessive menstruation and externally to treat burns, cuts, sores, and sore throats. The whole plant infusion used as a gargle for ulcers of the mouth and throat (GR). Make a tea

with 1 teaspoon of the dried whole aerial parts of the plant to 1 cup of water as a remedy for diarrhea and unspecified gynecological disorders. Dried aerial parts infused into tea to treat sore throat (CM). Consult with a professional holistic health-care professional for specific formulations and applications.

Note: Locate this plant to your garden so you have it on-site and handy when you need it.

JIMSONWEED, DATURA
**Solanaceae (*Datura stramonium* L.; *D. discolor* Bernh.*)*

Datura seed capsule

Identification: A 3'–4' annual with toothed leaves, coarse textured with distinctive trumpetlike flowers, white to light violet. Stem is hollow, upright, and branched. Seed capsule studded with spines. Leaves are long stemmed and coarse textured. Pungent (musty) odor when crushed.

Habitat: *D. stramonium* is found along roadsides, disturbed ground, and in bean and corn fields throughout the United States. *Datura meteloides,* more common in the Southwest and Four Corners area of Utah, is a popular, showy garden flower throughout the Midwest. The plant is an unusual example of the "doctrine of signatures" (or, like cures like): With all its spines, the plant screams, "Stay away!"

Food: Not used as food; toxic.

Traditional uses: This plant is Native American Big Medicine. The whole plant, especially the seeds, contains the alkaloids atropine and scopolamine. Atropine was used traditionally to dilate pupils. Leaves were smoked by Native Americans to treat asthma and other respiratory conditions. Smoking the leaves may also induce hallucinations. Numerous Indian nations used the plant as a ceremonial medicine. In a ritual that initiated young men into adulthood, datura roots powdered and taken as a hallucinogen and narcotic, reportedly to transform the user into a powerful animal. Powdered leaves mixed with grease and used as an ointment, analgesic, and disinfectant. The whole plant used symbolically to divine cures for disease and as a wash for cuts, wounds, and swellings. A paste of the plant applied to insect bites, snake envenomation, and spider bites. Pioneers and folk practitioners prepared the seeds and leaves as an expectorant to treat asthma, bronchitis, and the flu.

Modern uses: Atropine from datura is a sedative to the parasympathetic nerves; proprietary formulations are used to treat secondary symptoms of Parkinson's disease (Hyson, Johnson, and Jog 2002). Scopolamine patches are commercially available to treat motion sickness, dizziness, and seasickness (GR), as well as asthma. Homeopathic practitioners use a preparation to treat cramps, eye inflammations, and infection. In China, datura is still smoked to manage pain, treat asthma, and relieve arthritis.

Notes: This is a hallucinogen used by teenagers in rural areas—potentially fatal, and the toxic dose varies from plant to plant. The "get high" dose of swallowed seeds is close to the lethal dose. This herb and its extracts should be used only under medical supervision. It is a potent hallucinogen (Meuninck 2014).

CAUTION: Dry mouth, intoxication, dilated pupils, perhaps reddening of face and neck, delirium, hallucinations, tachycardia, and elevated blood pressure are symptoms of a severe overdose; as few as 20 seeds may lead to death.

High THC hybrid marijuana buds

MARIJUANA, WEED, HEMP, GANJA, REEFER, POT, PANAMA RED

Cannabaceae (*Cannabis sativa* L.)

Identification: Small to large plant. Potent hybrids are smaller. Leaves are 5-bladed, serrated (toothed) leaflets. Plant has a tough fibrous stem.

Habitat: Subtropical and temperate, wild strain is drought tolerant and will grow equally well on drained and marshy wet soils. In Michigan, marijuana before legalization was typically grown in canvas or coarse fiber grain sacks or flour bags stuffed with compost, and then placed atop rich wetland earth (or any other somewhat inaccessible area where plants can be hidden). It grows wild along railroad rights-of-way. I have found it in the weeds alongside factories where workers smoked; discarded seeds were left to grow.

Food: Oil decoctions mixed with various baked dishes.

Traditional uses: Cherokee used it as a stimulant, improving mental attitude in sick patients, giving them the will to go on and get well. This mild sedative appeared to help soldiers deal with Vietnam War; Vietnam protesters used the drug for the same reason. While I was working for the Department of Defense (DOD) in Asia and Europe, the drug (typically Turkish blond and black hashish) was readily available and openly used by officers and enlisted men.

Modern uses: Herbal and culinary preparations from flower heads have antiemetic, antinausea and, analgesic effects; bronchial dilator, somewhat antiasthmatic, and used traditionally to treat gout, malaria, forgetfulness, beriberi, constipation, and anxiety. In Europe, it is used externally in balms and as a poultice for wounds, pain, soreness, and infections. Also smoked or eaten to treat insomnia, arthritis, epilepsy, asthma bronchitis, whooping cough, and polyneuropathy. Eating the prepared drug circumvents the rasping, irritating effect of inhaling the hot smoke. In modern medical practice, marijuana is used to treat pain and symptoms of cancer, ulcers, emphysema, bronchitis, anxiety, hysteria, and neurasthenia. My mother, who suffered from increased inner ocular pressure, might have benefited from cannabis, but its use at the time in Michigan was illegal. A commercial cannabis derivative is available as an appetite stimulant for anorexia, loss of appetite due to cancer, and as an antiemetic caused by cancer treatments. The drug is also favored by AIDs patients.

CAUTION: Marijuana, an illegal drug in many states, should not be use while driving or operating machinery. Tetrahydrocannabinol (THC) studies suggest may induce reversible impotency after long and continued use. Chronic use may cause symptoms similar to chronic cigarette smoking such as bronchitis and laryngitis. Like most drugs, pregnant and nursing mothers should avoid the using the drug (see Meuninck, *Basic Illustrated Poisonous and Psychoactive Plants*, 72-73, 2014).

MOTHERWORT

Lamiaceae *(Leonurus cardiaca* L.)
Identification: Perennial in the mint family. Erect to 3½' in height, often shorter. Stem is quadrangular, grooved, usually hairy and hollow. Leaves are opposite on long petiole; leaves deeply lobed, coarsely toothed; upper leaves with 3–5 lobes, dark green on top, light green underneath. Small red flowers present in dense false whorls in the upper leaf axils. Plant flowers from April through August, depending on latitude

Leonurus cardiaca

and altitude. When crushed, plant leaves have unusual smell. The forked leaves are distinctive.
Habitat: Introduced and has spread nationwide through waste ground, roadsides, and edges of lawns. Commonly invasive in gardens.
Food: Although not considered a food, a few holistic practitioners consume the seeds for their beta-carotene and essential fatty acids content.
Traditional uses: Traditionally used by the Chinese and by pioneers to tone heart muscle (*Leonurus cardiaca* means "lion's heart"). Used as a tonic for treating amenorrhea, dysmenorrhea, urinary cramps, and general weakness, and reportedly clears toxins from the body. Ancient Greeks used the herb with pregnant women to treat stress and anxiety, but modern herbalists warn women against using the herb during pregnancy because of its uterine-stimulating effects. Plant traditionally used for stemming bacterial and fungal infections, both internally and externally. Whole aerial parts (leaves, flowers, stems) were gathered when the plant was in bloom, and the infusion was used to treat asthma and heart palpitations.
Modern uses: Homeopathic practitioners use minute fractions of the herb to treat flatulence, cardiac complaints, and hyperthyroidism (*PDR for Herbal Medicines* 2007, 586). Commission E–approved for nervous heart complaints (palpitations) and thyroid dysfunction. Homeopathic preparations treat menopause. The plant, considered by many herbalists and naturopaths as a superior woman's herb, is a documented uterine and circulatory stimulant that may relieve PMS; there is a long Chinese history and European folk history as such; although not hard science, the test of time strongly suggests it works. Conversely, it is hypotensive, antispasmodic, and diuretic; it works as a laxative, a sedative, and an emmenagogue (stimulating blood flow to the pelvic area and uterus) (GR). Leonurine in the plant tones the uterine membrane (membrane regulation). A homeopathic physician friend has used motherwort and passionflower to lower blood pressure with his patients.

Chinese practitioners use the herb as a single ingredient and do not typically compound it with other herbs. *L. japonica* is widely used in China and documented effective in numerous clinical studies. The aqueous decoction is antibacterial (*Barefoot Doctors Manual*, Running Press, 1977, 841)(GR). Chinese treat nephritis with aqueous extract made with 180–240 g of fresh herb in 1 L of water in decoction.

Notes: Folklore predicts, if there is a women residing in the home, motherwort appears magically to provide medicine. It transplants readily as long as you get the entire woody root.

CAUTION: Eating plant parts may be uterine stimulating; avoid if pregnant or lactating.

Verbascum thapsis

MULLEIN
Scrophularaceae *(Verbascum thapsis* L.)

Identification: A biennial to 6′ in height, flower spike borne on a stout, tall stem that arises from a base whorl of woolly leaves. Leaves to 15″ in length, ovate, covered with gray hair; basal leaves larger; clasping upper leaves less dense, smaller. Flowers yellow, ¾″–1″, 5 petals, densely packed on a spike at apex of the stem. Leaves are slimy and bitter when boiled.

Habitat: Nationwide in waste ground, roadsides, fields, edges of yards, and railroad rights-of-way.

Food: I have eaten the flowers sparingly in salads and tasted the tea, a practice I may once again employ, as I have occasional throat irritation.

Traditional uses: Drink leaf tea to treat upper respiratory tract conditions, coughs, congestion, and infections. Used for treating bronchitis and tracheitis. Leaf and flower infusion used to reduce and thin mucus formation. Dried leaves smoked to stop hiccups and to induce coughing up of phlegm (expectorant). Mullein can be combined with other expectorants, such as thyme (*Thymus vulgaris*) and coltsfoot (*Tussilago farfara*). Native Americans made a necklace of the roots to be worn by teething babies. Decoction of leaves was used for colds; a raw, crushed-leaf poultice was applied over wounds and painful swellings, and the mucilaginous leaves were rubbed over rashes. Mullein reported helpful in reducing pain from stinging nettle.

Modern uses: Flower is an Appalachian folk remedy for treating necrotic ulcer caused by a brown recluse spider bite: Folk practitioners pounded flowers into a blend of vinegar and Epsom salts and washed the bite 10 or 12 times per day. Therapeutic teas are available over the counter. Use leaf tea for respiratory congestion (GR). It is Commission E–approved for bronchitis and coughs. Flowers infused in olive oil are used in Europe to treat hemorrhoids and ear infections.

Notes: Add a couple plants to your yard. Simply find a first year's growth—a basal rosette of fuzzy leaves—dig it out, and transplant. The next year the biennial will bloom. The flower is striking. My spouse, Jill, suffers from allergies and asthma. She has used the tea of mullein leaf as an antispasmodic. Pour 1 cup of boiling water over 1 tablespoon of dried, crushed, or powdered leaves; when room temperature, strain and drink.

PASSIONFLOWER
Passifloraceae *(Passiflora incarnata L.)*

Passiflora *species*

Identification: Numerous varieties (500 species), all somewhat similar. Plant is a perennial vine, a woody stem climbing to 30′ or more with longitudinally striated (cracked) bark when mature. Leaves alternate, with petioles, serrated with fine hairs on both top and bottom; underside of leaf is hairier. Leaf blades have bumps called floral nectaries. Flowers single, striking, to 5″ in width, wheel shaped.

Habitat: Worldwide distribution; numerous species found across 7 climactic zones. A climbing vine is found wild in open areas and the forest edge of the southeastern United States. Most species are tropical or subtropical but will grow in a temperate garden and are often introduced.

Food: The leaf and flower tea has mild sedative properties. In some varieties, the fresh fruit is consumed raw or juiced. Mexicans mix passionflower blossoms and leaves with cornmeal or flour and eat it as a gruel. Native Americans ate leaves. Typically, leaves are parboiled and then panfried in vegetable oil or animal fat.

Traditional uses: Traditionally used in herbal medicine as a sleep aid (in cases of restlessness or insomnia due to mental stress) (CM).Pioneers used the whole plant with Epsom salts as a sedative bath. Root decoction and aerial parts made into tea and applied to hemorrhoids. Fresh or dried aerial parts or the whole herb were used in infusion as a mild sedative. Antispasmodic effect of the infusion is a gastro-intestinal aid. People used the infusion of crushed root for treating earache. They also pounded the root and applied the mass as a poultice on inflamed contusions, boils, and cuts. The root water of the plant was mixed with lye-treated corn to wean babies. The tisane was considered a blood purifier for many tribes.

Modern uses: Used by holistic practitioners to treat depression and for treating hysteria (unproven) (GR). Commission E–approved for treating nervousness and insomnia. In animal studies, the infusion is reported as sedative and antispasmodic; it inhibited motility of parasitic organisms (GR).

Notes: The "doctrine of signatures," that like cures like, suggests this sensual-looking plant is an aphrodisiac. *Passiflora* contains small amounts of beta-carboline harmala alkaloids that are monoamine oxidase inhibitors (MAOI) with antidepressant properties. Typically, the flower has only traces of the chemicals, but the leaves and the roots of some species are used to enhance the effects of mind-altering drugs.

PLANTAIN
Plantaginaceae *(Plantago lanceolata* L.; *P. major* L.; *P. maritima* L.*)*

Plantago maritima

Plantago major

Identification: Several varieties found across the United States. Leaves are in a basal whorl and the flower stem height may reach 8"–10". The difference is in the leaves: *P. major* leaves are broad, ovate; *P. lanceolata* leaves are long, narrow, and lance shaped.

Habitat: Nationwide in open ground, wasteland, lawns, edges of fields and roads, and lawns. Locate *P. maritima* in the upper tidal zone, often stem deep in water at high tide.

Food: In the spring pluck whole leaves and chop them into salads, or sauté with wild leeks, nettles, and watercress. Tear out the tough midleaf vein (rib) from summer and autumn leaves before adding them to salads.

Traditional uses: Strip off flowering heads by running the stem between thumb and forefinger. Add the flower heads to hot water to form a mucilaginous drink for treating constipation. A few believe that this plant, when crushed and applied to the skin, is a good antidote or treatment for poison ivy. Native Americans chewed the leaves to produce an antiseptic and immune-stimulating poultice for wounds, scrapes, cuts, and bruises. The poultice stops blood flow (styptic). You can use plantain the same way today; simply chew the plantain, masticating its chemistry with saliva containing defensin, a naturally occurring antibiotic in our mouth, and then fix the mastication over the wound. Digestive enzymes in our saliva are also weakly antimicrobial. Plantain lotions and ointments are used to treat hemorrhoids, skin fistulas, and ulcers. The tea is a diuretic, decongestant, and expectorant, and may be helpful in treating diarrhea, dysentery, irritable bowel syndrome, laryngitis, and urinary tract bleeding. Acubin from plantain increases uric acid excretion by kidneys and may be helpful in treating gout.

Modern uses: The tea of the fresh leaves is used to treat respiratory-tract infections and is considered antibacterial (GR). Commission E reports *P. lanceolata* extract from the fresh plant fights colds (4 g of herb to 1 cup boiling water), may alleviate symptoms of bronchitis and cough, and may reduce fever. It is Commission

E–approved for treating inflammation of the pharynx and mouth, skin inflammations colds, coughs, fever, and bronchitis. Typical dose is 3–6 g of the fresh whole
herb (aerial parts when in bloom) added to 1 cup of water just off the boil. Let it
cool, strain away plant material, then drink 3 or 4 times a day.

Notes: *Plantago* seeds of India and Africa are dried and used as a bulking laxative. *P.
ovata* is a constituent of Metamucil.

RED CLOVER
Fabaceae *(Trifolium pratense* L.)*

Identification: Perennial 12"–18"
in height, typically smaller on
poor ground. Three leaves with
distinct V marking on each leaflet.
Leaflets are fine toothed, ovate.
Flowers pink to red, dome shaped
or rounded in a dense terminal
cluster.

Habitat: Nationwide in fields,
roadsides, and waste ground. Prefers full sun.

Trifolium pratense

Food: Red clover makes a relaxing
floral tea; infuse tea from the fresh or dried flower. Toss florets in salad.

Traditional uses: Isoflavone estrogen-like compounds in clover are still used to
treat menopausal and postmenopausal problems. Dried flower heads are considered anticancer and are part of the Essiac anticancer formula, which include red clover, sheep sorrel, burdock root, slippery elm bark, rhubarb root, watercress, blessed
thistle, and kelp. Floral tea was used as a cure-all. Decoction or tea was used as an
external wash on burns, wounds, and insect bites. Pioneers claimed that drinking
the tea was an invigorating tonic that purified the blood. Tea was considered an
expectorant and therapy for respiratory problems such as asthma, bronchitis, and
whooping cough, and as an antispasmodic and mild sedative. Red clover was also
used as a wash for psoriasis and eczema.

Modern uses: Drug formulations of red clover isoflavones reduce frequency of hot
flashes (for more information see *PDR for Herbal Medicines* 2007, 694–695). A red-
clover isoflavone concentrate in tablet form (from flower heads) reduced bone loss
in a double-blind placebo-controlled trial with 177 women between the ages of
49 and 65 (Atkinson et al. 2004). A smaller trial showed that red-clover derivatives
reduced hot flashes (Van de Weijeer and Barentsen 2002). A third study showed a 23
percent increase in arterial blood flow to the heart in women (Nestel, Pomeroy, and
Kay 1999). Red clover is still used to treat menopausal symptoms and may improve
blood flow in the heart (GR). Trials are ongoing with red clover extract to improve
bone density and as a heart protector improving systemic arterial compliance.

Notes: Use floral teas sparingly unless supervised by a holistic health-care
professional.

CAUTION: Use a standardized red clover extract and then only under the supervision of licensed health-care practitioner. The drug may increase bleeding and has
other side effects.

SAINT-JOHN'S-WORT

Hyperacaceae *(Hypericum perforatum* L.; *Hypericum prolificum* L.)*

Hypericum perforatum

Identification: Stiff, tough stem, reddish and erect; may grow to 4' in height. Leaves ovate to lance shaped, attached at the base and covered by glands. Hold leaves toward the sun and you will see the glands; they appear as small perforations in the leaf—this indicates the species. Stems bear yellow flowers in terminal cymes (clusters). Five sepals are marked with numerous glands. Blossoms have numerous stamens fused into 3 bundles. Cylindrical seeds are less than ⅛" in length, elongated, black or brown, covered with small wart-like markings. *H. prolificum* is shrubby to 3' tall.

Habitat: Nationwide on roadsides, waste ground, fields, vacant lots, and prairies. There are numerous garden varieties.

Food: Not eaten.

Traditional uses: Used for 2,000 years, initially in Greece, to drive out evil spirits. The whole-plant decoction was used to induce abortions by promoting menstruation. Parts used included the fresh and dried flowers, buds, and leaves. Topical applications rubbed on sores may have antiviral, anti-

Shrubby Saint-John's-wort, Hypericum prolificum

bacterial, and wound-healing activity. Traditionally an anti-inflammatory, antibacterial, antiviral, antidiarrheal, and astringent agent. Flower infusion or flower tincture said to calm nerves, relieve insomnia, and boost mood by dispelling lethargy. Internally, tea used as a PMS treatment. Tea, standardized capsule, and tincture used to treat sciatica, anxiety, shingles, and fibrositis. Chewed root used as a snakebite remedy. Crushed leaves and flowers are stuffed in nostrils to stem nosebleed.

Modern uses: Several studies in Europe show the benefit of this herb to treat mild depression. A standardized extract of 0.3 percent hypericin, 300 mg, 3 times a day, found comparable in antidepressant effect to a drug standard of imipramine (see CM for recommended dosage). A recent study suggests a 5 percent hyperforin extract of the plant showed a slight increase in cognitive function. Other trials suggest that the drug may combat fatigue, relieve anxiety, improve sleep, help with weight loss, and attenuate menopausal symptoms (NIH). One study showed it relieved some forms of atopic dermatitis but was no more effective than placebo for treating major depression. It may work better than fluoxetine in treating depression (Fava et al. 2005). Commission E–approved for anxiety, skin inflammations, blunt injuries, wounds, burns, and mood enhancement (depression).

An external infusion of flowers and leaves is drunk as a cooling, astringent, wound-healing infection fighter. Aerial parts of plant infused into oil are applied topically to abrasions and bruises (CM). It is antiviral and anti-inflammatory and is said to promote healing when used externally as a poultice or wash for infections, burns, bruises, sprains, tendonitis, sprains, neuralgia, or cramps. In vitro studies show a widespread antimicrobial activity against influenza, herpes simplex I and II, retrovirus, polio virus, Sindbis virus, murine cytomegalovirus, hepatitis C, and gram-negative and gram-positive bacteria. It appears that exposure to ultraviolet light increases its antimicrobial activity.

Preparations are available over the counter as a dietary supplement or topical application. Check with your health practitioner for appropriate use and dosage.
Note: I have used both a decoction and tincture of the whole plant to treat psoriasis with no success.
CAUTION: Do not use to treat severe depression or bipolar depression. When used in German trials, extracts induced side effects in 2.4 percent of the test group; side effects included gastrointestinal irritation, restlessness, and mild allergic reactions. Studies suggest the chronic long-term use (abuse) of Saint-John's-wort is undesirable and may have negative health consequences. Purchase prepared products only after consultation with your health-care professional.

STINGING NETTLE

Urticaceae *(Urtica dioica* L.)
Identification: An erect perennial that grows to 5' on a square, grooved stem, studded with stinging hairs. Leaves are dark green, rough, lance to slightly oval shaped, toothed. Green flowers born in leaf axils, bearing numerous green seeds.
Habitat: Nationwide at edges of fields, streamside, wetlands, marshy areas, fringe areas, wasteland, and roadsides nationwide.
Food: Pick young shoots in fall (new growth) and steam, sauté, or stir-fry. One favorite recipe is to cream nettle into soup. For older, summer-hardened nettles, chop and simmer with other herbs (rosemary, celery, thyme, onions, leeks, and lovage) to make a vegetable bouillon or soup base. Discard the plant material after simmering for 25 minutes, and then use the broth in cooking. Pick top whorl of leaves and plant will bifurcate, doubling your harvest next time around.
Traditional uses: Nettles, a mineral-rich plant food, has been used for generations to treat allergies. The infusion of the aerial parts has expectorant qualities and was used for asthma and cough. Nettle tincture still used for flu, colds, pneumonia, and bronchitis. Dried plant is styptic when applied to wounds, and naturopaths use the drug to treat internal bleeding. According to Brill and Dean (1994) drinking nettle tea and eating nettles may make your skin clearer and healthier, and it may be therapeutic for eczema. Eating nettles may improve color, texture, gloss, and health of

Urtica dioica

hair. Aerial parts infused and used to treat urinary tract infections, kidney and bladder stones, and rheumatism. Root tincture used for irritable bladder and prostate complaints.

In traditional Russian medicine, nettle was used to treat hepatitis. In Spanish traditional medicine, nettle leaves prepared in infusion as a diuretic, to replenish minerals, as a hemostat, and purgative to remove toxins from the body. The root reportedly reduces the size of kidney stones. A decoction of the seeds used to prevent involuntary urination in children.

Stinging nettle is said to be helpful on arthritic joints as a counterirritant. Nettles used to thrash arthritic joints provides temporary relief (counterirritant). Mexican truck drivers use the plant to relieve sciatica; they also drink copious amounts of tequila. If you use the nettle arthritis remedy, have the tequila ready. Scarification (thrashing, pricking, or cutting the skin) is another way Native Americans treated arthritis; for details, view the DVD *Native American Medicine and Little Medicine* (Meuninck, Clark, and Roman 2007).

Modern uses: Nettle root and saw palmetto have been combined successfully to treat prostate enlargement (Engelmann et al. 2006). Commission E–approved for treating benign prostatic hyperplasia (BPH). Nettle roots in Russia tinctured for hepatitis and gallbladder inflammation. Investigations in Germany and in the United States seek to confirm nettle root extract as a treatment for prostate problems (GR) (CM).

A randomized study of arthritis sufferers suggests that stinging nettle extract, when accompanied by a lowered dose of the anti-inflammatory drug diclofenac (an anti-inflammatory drug for treating arthritis) improved or enhanced the efficacy of the prescription drug (Chrubasik et al. 1997; Ramm et al. 1996).

Notes: Stinging nettle grows readily in gardens, providing minerals, vitamins, and health-protecting phytochemistry. If you cannot obtain fresh nettle, buy freeze-dried. Rub out the sting of nettle with the juice of spotted touch-me-not (jewelweed, *Impatiens capensis*).

YARROW

Asteraceae *(Achillea millefolium L.)*

Identification: Spreading perennial, 1 to several stems attached to a spreading rhizome. Found in colonies and as individual plants; grows 3'–4' high on straight stem bearing soft, featherlike leaves. Fragrant! White flowers in flat clusters; each flower has 5 petal-like rays.

Habitat: Broadly distributed nationwide on roadsides, fields, yards, gardens, and edges of woods; drought tolerant.

Food: Not considered a food; see Notes.

Traditional uses: Yarrow tea is astringent and used to treat internal and external bleeding (styptic), and to treat conditions causing bloody urine such as kidney and bladder infections. Tea made from the aerial parts (leaves and flowers) is said to increase perspiration and reduce inflammation; it is used both externally and internally, externally on wounds and as a wash. Chinese take the tea to protect against thrombosis after stroke and use over wounds and for hemorrhoids, inflamed eyes, nosebleeds, and ulcers. Native Americans have infused the aerial parts of the plant to treat acute infections (colds, fever, flu), as a diuretic, to control coughing, and as a wash for bites, stings, and snakebites. Root decoction was a wash for pimples. Leaves infused and used to induce sleep, to treat poison ivy, alleviate diarrhea, and to reduce fever (febrifuge). Leaves

Achillea millefolium

were dried, crushed, and snorted as snuff for headaches or placed in the nose to stop bleeding. Fresh or dry leaves applied as a poultice over wounds or breast (nipple) abscesses. Leaf decoction was a hair rinse. Bella Coola peoples chewed leaves and applied them as a poultice to treat burns and boils. Leaves and flowers in decoction used for chest pains. Poultice of masticated flowers used to reduce edema. Leaves mixed with animal grease used as a poultice on chest and back to treat bronchitis. Juice or decoction of aerial parts considered a general tonic.

Modern uses: In Europe, the entire plant is used as an antispasmodic, emmenagogue (stimulates blood flow to pelvic area and uterus), tonic, carminative, digestive aid, and for wound healing. Wound healing facilitated by an infusion in distilled water and application as a wash to the wound site (GR). Most wound-healing preparations are oils or salves. Commission E–approved to treat loss of appetite, liver and gallbladder complaints, and dyspepsia.

Notes: Nettle is used to flavor many liqueurs, and decoction is gargled for sore throats. This attractive and useful herb should be in everyone's garden. Yarrow is one of the secret ingredients in fine beers. The bitter tea is a good digestive and anti-inflammatory that may protect you against infection. I use lard for an oil extraction from this herb because lard penetrates deeper into the skin than plant-based oils.

CAUTION: Drinking the tea and applying the herb can increase sensitivity to light (photosensitivity). The tea may contain a small amount of thujone, a carcinogen and liver toxin. Allergic reactions are possible, which is true of all plants. Due to its uterine-stimulating propensity, do not take yarrow internally while pregnant or nursing.

Appendix A: My Top Eleven Edible Garden Herbs

Use these herbs liberally when cooking: in salads and salad dressings, teas, barbecue, soups. Experiment! Taste the herb, imagine what it may complement, then give it a try.

1. Garlic: infection fighter, stimulant

2. Rosemary: cancer-fighting antioxidants, stimulant

3. Basil: antioxidants, infection fighter

4. Mint: stimulant, digestive

5. Lemon balm: relaxing tonic for mild depression, irritability, anxiety

6. Fennel: anti-inflammatory, analgesic, appetite stimulant, antiflatulent

7. Lovage: respiratory and digestive tonic, antibronchitis

8. Oregano: antiseptic, antiflatulent, stimulates bile and stomach acid, antiasthmatic

9. Cilantro (coriander): treats flatulence, bloating and cramps; breath sweetener

10. Horseradish: perspirant, stimulant

11. Thyme: tea for preventing altitude sickness, antiseptic, inhalant (antiasthmatic), stimulant

Appendix B: Helpful Websites

ars-grin.gov/duke. Database of medicinal plant chemistry

cinim.org. Canadian Institute of Natural and Integrative Medicine website

clinicaltrials.gov. Online source of clinical trials in progress with broad coverage

herbalgram.org. American Botanical Council website

herbvideos.com. Jim Meuninck's site with thousands of pages with photos and links

nccam.nih.gov. US Office of Alternative and Complementary Medicine website

rain-tree.com. Database of Amazon rain forest plants and their medicinal uses

Appendix C: References and Resources

Aller, Wilma. "Aboriginal Food Utilization of Vegetation by Indians of the Great Lakes Region as Recorded in the Jesuit Relations," *Wisconsin Archaeologist* 35 (1954): 59–73.

Atkinson C., J. Compston, N. E. Day, M. Dowsett, and S. A. Bingham. "The Effects of Phytoestrogen Isoflavones on Bone Density in Women: A Double-Blind Randomized, Placebo-Controlled Trial," *American Journal of Clinical Nutrition* 79, no. 2 (2004): 326–33.

Balbaa, S. I., A. Y. Zaki, S. M. Abdel-Wahab, E. S. el-Denshary, and M. Motazz-Bellah. "Preliminary Phytochemical and Pharmacological Investigations of the Roots of Different Varieties of *Cichorium intybus*," *Planta Medica* 24, no. 2 (October 1973): 133–44.

Barrett, S. A. "The Washo Indians," *Bulletin of the Public Museum of the City of Milwaukee* 2, no. 1 (1917): 1–52. **Note:** Search Google: Basehart Apache Indians.

Basehart, Harry. *Apache Indians XII: Mescalero Apache Subsistence Patterns and Socio-Political Organization*. New York: Garland Publishing, 1974.

Block, K. I., and M. N. Mead. "Immune System Effects of Echinacea, Ginseng, and Astragalus: A Review," *Integrative Cancer Therapies* 2, no. 3 (September 2003): 247–67.

Bradley, Will. "Medical Practices of New England Aborigines," *Journal of the American Pharmaceutical Association* 25, no. 2 (1936): 138–47.

Blumenthal, Mark, Alicia Goldberg, and Josef Brinckmann, eds. *Herbal Medicine: Expanded Commission E Monographs*. Austin, TX: American Botanical Council, 2000.

Blumenthal, M., et al., eds. *The Complete German Commission E Monographs: Therapeutic Guide to Herbal Medicines*. Translated by S. Klein and R. S. Rister. Austin, TX: American Botanical Council, 1998.

Brill, Steve, with Evelyn Dean. *Identifying and Harvesting Edible and Medicinal Plants in Wild (and Not So Wild) Places*. New York: Hearst Books, 1994.

Brown, Deni. *Encyclopedia of Herbs & Their Uses: The Definitive Guide to the Identification, Cultivation, and Use of 1,000 Herbs*. New York: Dorling Kindersley, 1995.

Campbell, T. "Medicinal Plants Used by Choctaw, Chickasaw, and Creek Indians in the Early Nineteenth Century," *Journal of the Washington Academy of Sciences* 41, no. 9 (1951): 285–90.

Carr, L., and C. Westey. "Surviving Folktales and Herbal Lore among the Shinnecock Indians," *Journal of American Folklore* 58 (1945): 113–23.

Chatterjee, M., P. Verma, and G. Palit. "Comparative Evaluation of *Bacopa monniera* and *Panax quniquefolium* in Experimental Anxiety and Depressive Models in Mice," *Indian Journal of Experimental Biology* 48, no. 3 (2010): 306–13.

Chevallier, Andrew. *Encyclopedia of Medicinal Plants: A Practical Reference Guide to over 550 Key Herbs and Their Medicinal Uses.* New York: DK Publishing, 1996.

Chrubasik, S., W. Enderlein, R. Bauer, and W. Grabner. "Evidence for Antirheumatic Effectiveness of Herba *Urticae dioicae* in Acute Arthritis: A Pilot Study," *Phytomedicine* 4, no. 2 (June 1997): 105–8.

Chung, K. T., T. Y. Wong, C. I. Wei, Y. W. Huang, and Y. Lin. "Tannins and Human Health: A Review," *Critical Reviews in Food Science and Nutrition* 38, no. 6 (1998): 421–64.

Circosta, C., F. Occhiuto, S. Ragusa, A. Trovato, G. Tumino, F. Briguglio, and A. De Pasquale. "A Drug Used in Traditional Medicine: *Harpagophytum procumbens* DC. II. Cardiovascular Activity," *Journal of Ethnopharmacology* 11 (1984): 259–74.

Continho, Henrique D. M., José G. M. Costa, Edeltrudes O. Lima, Vivyanne S. Falcão-Silva, and José P. Siqueira-Júnior. "Potentiating Effect of *Mentha arvensis* and Chlorpromazine in the Resistance to Aminoglycosides of Methicillin-Resistant *Staphylococcus aureus*," *In Vivo* 23, no. 2 (March–April 2009): 287–9.

Coothankandaswamy, Veena, et al. "The Alternative Medicine Pawpaw and Its Acetogenin Constituents Suppress Tumor Angiogenesis via the HIF-1/VEGF Pathway," *Journal of Natural Products* 73, no. 5 (2010): 956–61.

Coville, Frederick. "Notes on the Plants Used by the Klamath Indians of Oregon," *Contributions from the US National Herbarium* 5, no. 2 (June 9, 1897): 87–110.

Duke, James. *CRC Handbook of Medicinal Herbs.* Boca Raton, FL: CRC Press, 1985.

———. *Database of Phytochemical Constituents of GRAS Herbs and Other Economic Plants.* Boca Raton, FL: CRC Press, 1992.

———. *Handbook of Biological Active Phytochemicals and Their Activities.* Boca Raton, FL: CRC Press, 1992.

———. *Handbook of Edible Weeds.* Boca Raton, FL: CRC Press, Ann Arbor, 1992.

———. *Handbook of Northeastern Indian Medicinal Plants.* Lincoln, MA: Quarterman Publications, 1986.

Engelmann, U., C. Walther, B. Bondarenko, P. Funk, and S. Schläfke. "Efficacy and Safety of a Combination of *Sabal* and *Urtica* Extract in Lower Urinary Tract Symptoms," *Arzneimittel-Forschung / Drug Research* 56, no. 3 (2006): 222–9. See: www.ncbi.nlm.nih.gov/pubmed/16618015.

Fava, M., et al. "A double blind randomized trial of St. John's Wort, Fluoxetine, and Placebo in Major Depressive Disorder," *Journal of Clinical Psychopharmocology* 25, no. 5 (2005): 441–7.

Fewkes, Walter. "A Contribution to Ethnobotany," *American Anthropologist* A9, no. 1 (January 1896): 14–21.

Fletcher, Alice C., and Francis La Flesche. "The Omaha Tribe," *Twenty-Seventh Annual Report of the Bureau of American Ethnology to the Secretary of the Smithsonian Institution, 1905-6* (1911): 17–654.

Foster, Steven, and James A. Duke. *A Field Guide to Medicinal Plants: Eastern and Central North America.* Boston: Houghton Mifflin, 1990.

Gilmore, Melvin R. *Some Chippewa Uses of Plants.* Ann Arbor: University of Michigan Press, 1933.

———. *A Study in the Ethnobotany of the Omaha Indians.* Nebraska State Historical Society Collections, vol. 17 (1913): 314–57.

———. *Uses of Plants by the Indians of the Missouri River Region.* Washington, DC: Government Printing Office, 1949; https://archive.org/stream/usesofplantsbyin00gilm#page/n0/mode/2up.

Gunter, Erna. *Ethnobotany of Western Washington: The Knowledge and Use of Indigenous Plants by Native Americans.* Seattle: University of Washington Press, 1973.

Harrington, John. *Tobacco among the Karuk Indians of California.* Smithsonian Institution Bureau of American Ethnology, Bulletin 91. Washington, DC: Government Printing Office, 1932.

Hart, Jeff. *Montana Native Plants and Early Peoples.* Helena: Montana Historical Society Press, 1992.

Hassan, H. A., and M. I. Yousef. "Ameliorating Effect of Chicory (*Cichorium intybus* L.) in a Supplemented Diet against Nitrosamine Precursors That Induce Liver Injury and Oxidative Stress in Male Rats," *Food & Chemical Toxicology* 48 (August–September 2010): 2163–9.

Hsu Hong-Yen. *Oriental Materia Medica: A Concise Guide.* New Canaan, CT: Keats Publishing, 1986.

Hyson, H. C., A. M. Johnson, and M. S. Jog. "Sublingual Atropine for Sialorrhea Secondary to Parkinsonism: A Pilot Study," *Movement Disorders* 17, no. 6 (2002): 1318–20.

Kapoor, L. D. *Handbook of Ayurvedic Medicinal Plants.* Boca Raton, FL: CRC Press, 1990.

Knott, A., et al. "Natural *Arctium lappa* Fruit Extract Improves the Clinical Signs of Aging Skin," *Journal of Cosmetic Dermatology* 7, no. 4 (December 2008): 281–9.

Króliczewska, Bozena, and Wojciech Zawadzki. "The Influence of Skullcap Root Addition (*Scutellaria baicalensis radix*) on Calcium, Inorganic Phosphorus, Magnesium, and Iron Levels in Broiler Chicken Serum," *Electronic Journal of Polish Agricultural Universities* 8, no. 3 (2005); www.ejpau.media.pl/volume8/issue3/abs-22.html.

Kucera, M., J. Kálal, and Z. Polesná. "Effects of Symphytum Ointment on Muscular Symptoms and Functional Locomotor Disturbances," *Advances in Therapy* 17, no. 4 (July–August 2000): 204–10.

Kuhnlein and Turner. *Traditional Plant Foods of Canadian Indigenous People.* Williston, VT: Gordon and Breach Science Publishers, 1991.

Lawrence Review of Natural Products. St. Louis, MO: Facts and Comparisons, 1993.

Mandelbaum, David. "The Plains Cree," *Anthropological Papers of the American Museum of Natural History* 37 (1940); www.amazon.com/The-Plains-Cree-Ethnographic-Comparative/dp/0889770131.

McGuffin, M., C. Hobbs, R. Upton, A. Goldberg, eds. *American Herbal Products Association's Botanical Safety Handbook.* Boca Raton, FL: CRC Press, 1997.

Memorial Sloan Kettering Cancer Center, 2014. "Information about Herbs, Botanicals, and Other Products." Accessed May 3, 2014; http://www.mskcc.org/cancer-care/integrative-medicine/about-herbs-botanicals-other-products.

Meuninck, Jim. *Basic Illustrated Edible Wild Plants and Useful Herbs.* Guilford, CT: Globe Pequot Press, 2013.

———. *Basic Illustrated Poisonous and Psychoactive Plants.* Guilford, CT: Globe Pequot Press , 2014.

———. *Herbal Odyssey*; www.herbvideos.com, 2007. CD-ROM.

———. *Little Medicine: The Wisdom to Avoid Big Medicine*; www.herbvideos.com, 2005. DVD.

———. *Medicinal Plants of North America: A Field Guide.* Guilford, CT: Globe Pequot Press, 2008.

Meuninck, Jim, and James Duke. *Edible Wild Plants*; www.herbvideos.com, 2007. DVD.

———. *Trees, Shrubs, Nuts & Berries.* www.herbvideos.com, 2007. DVD.

Meuninck, Jim, Patsy Clark, Theresa Barnes, and Estella Roman. *Native American Medicine and Little Medicine*; www.herbvideos.com, 2007. DVD.

Meuninck, Jim, et al. *Cooking with Edible Flowers and Culinary Herbs*; www.herbvideos.com, 2007. DVD.

Meuninck, Jim, et al. *Natural Health with Medicinal Herbs and Healing Foods*; www.herbvideos.com, 2007. DVD.

Corson and Meuninck———. *Diet for Natural Health: One Diet for Disease Prevention and Weight Control*; www.herbvideos.com, 2007. DVD.

Moerman, Daniel E. *Native American Ethnobotany.* Portland, OR: Timber Press, 1998.

Moore, Michael. *Medicinal Plants of the Mountain West.* Santa Fe, NM: Museum of New Mexico Press, 2003.

———. *Medicinal Plants of the Pacific West.* Santa Fe, NM: Red Crane Books, 1993.

Naegele, Thomas. *Edible and Medicinal Plants of the Great Lakes Region.* Davisburg, MI: Wilderness Adventure Books, 1996.

National Institute for the Control of Pharmaceutical and Biological Products and Lou Zhicen, eds. *Color Atlas of Chinese Traditional Drugs*. Beijing: Science Press, 1987.

Nestel, P. J., et al. "Isoflavones from Red Clover Improves Systemic Arterial Compliance but Not Plasma Lipids in Menopausal Women," *Journal of Clinical Endocrinology and Metabolism* 84, no. 3 (1999): 895–8.

Osterhoudt, K. C., S. K. Lee, J. M. Callahan, and F. M. Henretig. "Catnip and the Alteration of Human Consciousness," *Veterinary and Human Toxicology* 39, no. 6 (1997): 373–5.

Palmer, Gary. "Shuswap Indian Ethnobotany," *Syesis* 8 (1975): 29–51.

PDR for Herbal Medicines, 3rd ed. Montvale, NJ: Thomson Healthcare, 2005.

PDR for Herbal Medicines, 4th ed. Montvale, NJ: Thomson Healthcare, 2007.

Pojar, Jim, and Andy MacKinnon. *Plants of Coastal British Columbia*. Auburn, WA: Lone Pine Publishing,1994.

http://www.phytomedicinejournal.com/article/S0944-7113(97)80052-9/references.

Radhamani, T. R., L. Sudarshana, and R. Krishnan. "Defense and Carnivory: Dual Roles of Bracts in *Passiflora foetida*," *Journal of Biosciences* 20 (December 1995): 657–64.

Ramm, et al. "Brennesselblatter-extrakt bei arthrose und rheumatoider arthritis," *Therapiewoche* 28 (1996): 3–6; www.phytomedicinejournal.com/article/S0944-7113(97)80052-9/references.

Reed, Daniel. *Chinese Herbal Medicine*. Boston: Shambhala Publications, 1987.

Schwarz, E., A. Parlesak, H. H. Henneicke-von Zepelin, J. C. Bode, and C. Bode. "Effect of Oral Administration of Freshly Pressed Juice of *Echinacea purpurea* on the Number of Various Subpopulations of B- and T-lymphocytes in Healthy Volunteers: Results of a Double-Blind, Placebo-Controlled Cross-Over Study," *Phytomedicine* 12 (September 2005): 625–31.

Smith, Harlan. "Materia Medica of the Bella Coola and Neighboring Tribes of British Columbia," *National Museum of Canada Bulletin* 56 (1929): 47–68.

Stenkvist, B., et al. "Evidence of a Modifying Influence of Heart Glycosides on the Development of Breast Cancer," *Analytical & Quantitative Cytology & Histology* 2, no. 1 (1980): 49–54.

Tull, Delena. *Edible and Useful Plants of Texas and the Southwest: A Practical Guide*. Austin: University of Texas Press, 1999.

Van de Weijer, P. H., and R. Barentsen. "Isoflavones from Red Clover (Promensil) Significantly Reduce Menopausal Hot Flush Symptoms Compared with Placebo," *Maturitas* 42, no. 3 (July 2002): 187–93.

Vendrame, Stefano, Aleksandra S. Kristo, Dale A. Schuschke, and Dorothy Klimis-Zacasa. "Wild Blueberry Consumption Affects Aortic Vascular Function in the Obese Zucker Rat," *Applied Physiology, Nutrition, and Metabolism* 39, no. 2 (2014): 255-61.

Vestal, Paul. "Ethnobotany of the Ramah Navaho," *Papers of the Peabody Museum of American Archaeology and Ethnology, Harvard University* 40, no. 1 (1952): 1–94.

Vestal, Paul, and Richard Schultes. *The Economic Botany of the Kiowa Indians.* Cambridge, MA: Botanical Museum, 1939.

Vogel, Virgil. *American Indian Medicine.* Norman: University of Oklahoma Press, 1970.

Wang, H. Y., and Y. P. Chen, "Clinical Observation on Treatment of Diabetic Nephropathy with Compound Fructus Arctii Mixture" [in Chinese], *Zhongguo Zhong Xi Yi Jie He Za Zhi* 24, no. 7 (July 2004): 589–92.

Whitney, Steven. *Western Forests.* New York: Alfred A. Knopf, 1985.

Yanosky, Elias. *Food Plants of the North American Indians.* Washington, DC: US Department of Agriculture, 1936.

Zhu, D., J. Wang, Q. Zeng, Z. Zhang, and R. Yan. "A Novel Endophytic Huperzine A–Producing Fungus, *Shiraia* sp. Slf14, Isolated from *Huperzia serrata*," *Journal of Applied Microbiology* 109, no. 4 (October 2010): 1469–78.

Zicari, D., et al. "Diabetic Retinopathy Treated with Arnica 5CH Microdoses," *Investigative Ophthalmology & Visual Science* 39 (1998): 118.

Index

Achillea millefolium L., 70–72
Acorus calamus L., 41–42
Acorus calamus var. *americanus,* 42
Alnus rubra Bong., 10–11
alpine bistort, 4–5
American larch, 42–43
American mandrake, 22–23, 38
American yew, 14
Arctium lappa L., 50–51
arnica, 2–3
Arnica acaulis Walt, 2–3
Arnica cordifolia Hook, 2–3
Arnica latifolia Bong., 2–3
Arnica montana L., 2–3
arrowleaf, 3–4
Artemisia tridentata Nutt., 12–13
Asimina triloba L. Dunal., 25–26
aspen, 24–25

balm melissa, 48–49
Balsamorhiza sagittata Pursh Nutt., 3–4
balsam poplar, 24–25
balsamroot, 3–4
bee balm, 49–50
Betula alleghaniensis, 40
Betula papyrifera Marsh., 40–41
bilberry, 30–31
birch, 40–41
bistort, 4–5
bittersweet nightshade, 30
black walnut, 16
black willow, 44–45
bloodroot, 17
blueberry, 30–31
blue oak, 23–24
bog blueberry, 30–31
boneset, 31–32
buckthorn, 5
burdock, 50–51
bur oak, 23–24

calamus, 41–42
Cannabis sativa L., 62–63

cascara sagrada, 5
catnip, 52–53
chestnut oak, 23–24
chicory, 51–52
Cichorium intybus L., 51–52
climbing nightshade, 30
club moss, 32–33
Concord grapes, 20–21
cottonwood, 24–25
cranberry, 33–34
Crataegus spp., 21–22
curly dock, 53–54

dandelion, 54–55
datura, 61–62
Datura discolor Bernh., 61–62
Datura stramonium L., 61–62
devil's club, 5–6
Digitalis purpurea L., 58–59
dock, 53–54
Douglas fir, 6–7
duckweed, 34
dwarf ginseng, 17–18

echinacea, 55–56
Echinacea angustifolia DC., 55–56
Echinacea purpurea L. Moench, 55–56
elder/elderberry, 36–37
English yew, 14
ephedra, 7–8
Ephedra sinica Stapf, 7–8
Ephedra viridis Coville, 7–8
equisetum, 35
Equisetum arvense L., 35
Equisetum hyemale L., 35
Eupatorium perfoliatum L., 31–32
evening primrose, 56–57

flax, 57–58
foxglove, 58–59

Gambel oak, 23–24
ganja, 62–63

ginseng, 17–18
gobo burdock, 50–51
goldenrod, 59–60
goldenseal, 19
grapes, 20–21
grapeseed extract, 20–21
Gray es. Miq, 5–6
greater water dock, 53–54

Hamamelis virginiana L., 27
hawthorn, 21–22
heal-all, 60–61
hemp, 62–63
horsemint, 49–50
horsetail, 35
huperzia, 32–33
Huperzia lucidula (Michx) Trevisan,
    32–33
Huperzia selago L., 32–33
Hydrastis canadensis L., 19
Hypericum perforatum L., 68–69
Hypericum prolificum L., 68–69

Impatiens capensis Meerb., 37–38

jewelweed, 37
jimsonweed, 61–62
joint fir, 7–8
Juglans nigra L., 16
juniper, 8–9
Juniperus communis L., 8–9

Larix decidua, 43
Larix larcina Du Boi, K. Koch., 42–43
Larix occidentalis, 43
Lemna gibba, 34
Lemna minor L., 34
lemon balm, 48–49
Leonurus cardiaca L., 63–64
leopard's bane, 2–3
linseed, 57–58
Linum usitatissimum L., 57–58
lobelia, 38–39
Lobelia siphilitica L., 38–39

Mahonia acqifolium (Pursh) Nutt.,
    9–10

Mahonia nervosa Pursh Nutt. var.
    nervosa, 9–10
ma huang, 7–8
marijuana, 62–63
mayapple, 22–23, 38
meadow bistort, 4–5
Melissa officinalis L., 48–49
Mentha arvensis, 39–40
Mentha piperita L., 39–40
mint, 39–40
Monarda didyma L., 49–50
Monarda fistulosa L., 49–50
Mormon tea, 7–8
motherwort, 63–64
mountain tobacco, 2–3
mullein, 64–65

Nasturtium officinale L., 43–44
Nepeta cataria L., 52–53
nettle, 69–70

oak, 23–24
Oenothera biennis L., 56–57
Oplopanax hirridus Sm. Torr., 5–6
Oregon grape, 9–10
Oregon white oak, 23–24

Pacific yew, 14
Panama red, 62–63
Panax ginseng C.A. Meyer, 17–18
Panax quinquefolius L., 17–18
Panax trifolius, 17–18
paper birch, 40–41
Passiflora incarnata L., 65
passionflower, 65
pawpaw/papaw, 25–26
peppermint, 39–40
Persicaria bistortoides Pursh., 4–5
Persicaria vivaparum L., 4–5
Plantago lanceolata L., 66–67
Plantago major L., 66–67
Plantago maritima L., 66–67
plantain, 66–67
Podophyllum peltatum L., 22–23, 38
poplar, 24–25
Populus balsamifera L., 24–25
Populus deltoides Bartr. ex Marsh, 24–25

Populus tremuloides Michx., 24–25
pot, 62–63
Prunella vulgaris L., 60–61
Pseudotsuga menziesii Mirbel
    Franco, 6–7
purple coneflower, 55–56
purple foxglove, 58–59

Quercus alba, 23–24
Quercus spp., 23–24

red alder, 10–11
red cedar, 11–12
red clover, 67
red elm, 26
red Indian paint, 17
red puccoon, 17
reefer, 62–63
Rhamnus alnifolia (L.) Her., 5
Rhamnus purshiana (DC.) Cooper, 5
Rumex cripus L., 53–54
Rumex orbiculatus A. Gray, 53–54

sage/sagebrush, 12–13
Saint-John's-wort, 68–69
Salix alba L., 44–45
Salix nigra Marsh, 44
Salix spp., 44–45
Sambucus canadensis L., 36–37
Sambucus cerulean Raf., 36–37
Sambucus nigra (L.) *R. Bolli.*, 36–37
Sambucus racemosa L., 36–37
Sanguinaria canadensis L., 17
scouring rush, 35
self-heal, 60–61
Sitka valerian, 13–14
slippery elm, 26
Solanum dulcamara L., 30
Solidago canadensis L., 59–60
spotted touch-me-nots, 37–38
stinging nettle, 69–70
swamp chestnut oak, 23–24

swamp willow, 44–45
sweet flag, 41–42

tamarack, 42–43
Taraxacum officinale G. H. Weber ex
    Wiggers, 54–55
Taxus brevifolia Nutt., 14
thoroughwort, 31–32
Thuga plicata D. Don., 11–12
Thuja occidentalis, 12
Trifolium pratense L., 67

Ulmus rubra Muhl., 26
Urtica dioica L., 69–70

Vaccinium myrtillus L., 30–31
Vaccinium oxycossus L., 33–34
Vaccinium uliginosum L., 31
Valeriana officinalis L., 13–14
Valeriana sitchensis Bong., 13–14
Verbascum thapsis L., 64–65
Vitis labrusca L., 20–21
Vitis vinifera L., 20–21

watercress, 43–44
weed, 62–63
Western larch, 43
white birch, 40–41
white oak, 23–24
white willow, 44–45
wild bergamont, 49–50
willow, 44–45
wine, 20–21
witch hazel, 27
wolf's bane, 2–3

yarrow, 70–72
yellow birch, 40
yellow chestnut oak, 23–24
yellow dock, 53–54
yew, 14

About the Author

Jim Meuninck, naturalist and biologist, resides on Eagle Lake, Michigan, with his spouse, Jill. Jim has written and published numerous books, including four FalconGuides, two CDs, and six DVDs on ethnobotany, Native American medicine, edible flowers, and survival skills. For more information on the author and to access his vast reservoir of free botanical information and self-reliance tips, go to herbvideos.com.